NINETEEN CENTURIES OF
CHRISTIAN SONG

CHARLES WESLEY

NINETEEN CENTURIES
OF
CHRISTIAN SONG

BY
EDWARD S. NINDE, D.D.

FOREWORD BY
MARY NINDE GAMEWELL

28510

NEW YORK
Fleming H. Revell Company
LONDON AND EDINBURGH

New York: 158 Fifth Avenue
London: 21 Paternoster Square

To

MISS EMILY S. PERKINS

FOUNDER OF

THE HYMN SOCIETY OF AMERICA

FOREWORD

MY BROTHER'S interest in hymnody began in his college days at Wesleyan University, and continued with growing intensity through life. Never allowing this study to interfere with his regular pastoral work, he made it his hobby, to which he turned from time to time for relaxation. Knowing this, I was not surprised, in looking over his papers after his death, to find voluminous notes on his favorite theme taken from various sources in many libraries in this country and Great Britain.

He had once said to me that he planned to write a book on general hymnody, calling it "Nineteen Centuries of Christian Song," and making it much ampler and more inclusive than his work on "The Story of the American Hymn," published in 1921. His failing health, however, led me to think he had abandoned this purpose; so it was almost by accident that I found the material which is in the present volume. I now fully believe he wrote this abbreviated story out of an innate love for the study of hymnody which he could not resist, and with no idea whatever of publication. Yet, as I read the notes, they seemed to me to possess interest and value, not so much for those quite familiar with the history of hymnody as for others only slightly acquainted with the subject.

Many, no doubt, feel an interest in hymns who would not be apt to turn to a detailed, technical account for information. To this class—particularly to alert young people—the present brief, simple account of the development of Christian song may have an appeal, and it is solely with this hope in mind that the story is published. My brother's notes give clear indication of his thorough familiarity with the hymns of the Oxford Movement and of those that followed in the nineteenth century. Had he been able to carry out his original plan I am confident this part of the hymnic story would have received from him full and adequate treatment.

I owe a debt of gratitude to Mr. Carl F. Price for his kindness in reading and editing the manuscript and in advising in all matters pertaining to its publication.

Too much cannot be said of the help given by my husband, without whose sympathetic cooperation this work could not have been done.

MARY NINDE GAMEWELL.

CONTENTS

Hark! the herald angels sing,
"Glory to the newborn King!"

Jesus came to earth in an outburst of
song. He entered his Passion chanting
a hymn. Through life he was a lover
of song, and it is fitting that his followers should be a singing people.

I

HYMNS OF THE EARLY CHURCH

MAKING MELODY—to the Lord" was perfectly natural to the early Christians; they inherited the practice from a long line of Hebrew sires. We read of the rapturous Song of Deliverance which Moses and the men of Israel uttered after the passage of the Red Sea, when, to the accompaniment of timbrel and dance, Miriam and her women joined in with the refrain:

> Sing ye to the Lord, for he hath triumphed gloriously;
> The horse and his rider hath he thrown into the sea. Ex 15:1

In a similar strain Deborah and Barak sang of their victory over the mighty Sisera.

When Hannah, the mother of Samuel, looked into the face of her newborn babe, she broke into a hymn of gratitude to God: "My heart rejoiceth in the Lord;—I rejoice in thy salvation." 1st Sam 2:1

In a far different key sounds the noble dirge which David uttered for Saul and Jonathan: "The beauty of Israel is slain upon thy high places: how are the mighty fallen!"

It is, however, in that treasury of song, the Book of Psalms, that we find the most remarkable collection of sacred lyrics of any age or of any tongue. Scarcely possible is it to overestimate their influence on the religious life, not only of the Hebrew people, but also of the Christian Church. Byron spoke truly when he said that "David's lyre grew mightier than his throne." For hundreds of years this collection was the hymnal of the Jews, a fountain of spiritual instruction and comfort that never failed. It was a book that Jesus knew and loved, from which he sang and whose blessed words he often quoted. On that last night, when he met the Twelve in the upper chamber in Jerusalem, as he was about to pass into the darkness, he led the little company in a hymn. No doubt it was the group of Psalms 115-118, being the second part of the Hallel or Song of Praise, which the Jews were in the habit of chanting at the Passion meal.

From this noble heritage of ancient song, it was a natural and easy transition to the still more exalted hymnody of the Christian era. In celebrating the advent of the King, how beautiful and appropriate that men should join with angels in praise to God! The united minstrelsy of heaven and earth was none too glorious for such a time as this.

No wonder that when the young virgin of Nazareth received the marvelous tidings that she, of all the daughters of Israel, had been chosen to be the mother of the long-expected Messiah, she cried in ecstasy: *Luke 1:46*

> My soul doth magnify the Lord,
> And my spirit hath rejoiced in God my Saviour.

As if in answering echo, came the exultant strain from the unsealed lips of Zacharias, the aged priest, as he took in his arms the infant John:

> Blessed be the Lord God of Israel;
> For he hath visited and redeemed his people. *Luke 1:68*

But sublimest of all was the hymn of the heavenly host on the first Christmas night:

> Glory to God in the highest,
> And on earth peace, good will toward men.

Then, like a gracious benediction to their jubilant service of advent song, there fall upon our ears the words of the patriarchal Simeon:

> Lord, now lettest thou thy servant depart in peace,
>   According to thy word;
> For mine eyes have seen thy salvation.

These four hymns, known by their Latin names, the "Magnificat," the "Benedictus," the "Gloria in Excelsis" and the "Nunc Dimittis," very early found their way into the service of the Church, and have been in well-nigh universal use from that time to this. They help to remind us that, with all our divisions and differences, fundamentally the followers of Jesus are one.

The primitive Church had no distinctively Christian hymn book; and yet, both in private and in public worship, large use was made of religious song. Paul especially delighted in it, for he knew its value. On that memorable night when he and Silas lay in the dungeon at Philippi, feet in the stocks, backs bleeding, victims of cruel injustice, we can well imagine that it was the great apostle who proposed that they comfort their hearts by singing hymns; and no wonder, as the joyous notes rang out, "the prisoners were listening." Doubtless they caught at least a part of the meaning, for, as Paul once wrote to the Christians in Corinth, he had made it a practice to "sing with the understanding," so that people might know what he was saying. He likewise urged his fellow believers to make use of "psalms and hymns and spiritual songs, singing and making melody in your heart to the Lord." Probably he had in mind parts from the temple and synagogue service, with which every convert from Judaism would be familiar, and also simple hymns of Christian origin that already were beginning to appear among the disciples.

Scattered through the New Testament are sentences in rhythmic form which may be fragments of early Christian hymns. For example, it has been surmised that the lines,

> Awake, thou that sleepest,
> And arise from the dead,
> And Christ shall give thee light (Ephesians 5. 14),

are a part of a baptismal hymn. And in describing the "mystery of godliness" Paul seems to be quoting from an early saying or hymn:

> Manifest in the flesh,
> Justified in the Spirit,
> Seen of angels,
> Preached unto the Gentiles,
> Believed on in the world,
> Received up into glory. (I Timothy 3. 16)

In the Book of Revelation there occur a number of rhythmic passages which quite likely were sung by the early Christians, such as the "Song of Moses and of the Lamb":

> Great and marvelous are thy works,
>   O Lord God the Almighty!
> Righteous and true are thy ways,
> Thou King of the ages.
> Who shall not fear, O Lord,
>   And glorify thy name?
>   For thou only art holy;
> For all the nations shall come
> And worship before thee;
> For thy righteous acts
> Have been made manifest.   (Revelation 15. 3, 4.)

It is interesting to find that outside of the New Testament, the earliest response to singing among the Christians comes not from one of their own number, but from a Roman official. In the year 109 A.D., during the reign of the Emperor Trajan, and not long after the death of the Apostle John, Pliny the Younger was appointed governor of the province of Bithynia in Asia Minor. In one of his first reports he told the emperor of his contact with the curious sect of the Christians, and of how he had been solemnly assured that their worst offense was *in gathering before dawn on an appointed day*—no doubt Sunday—*to sing in responsive fashion hymns to Christ as God.* This brief allusion is of great importance not only as indicating the rapid spread of the Church, but also the prominent place of song and the manner of singing in Christian worship. Of those early hymns no definite trace remains, but we may readily suppose that they were similar to the rhythmic sentences already quoted. Doubtless disciples were often moved to express themselves in forms of praise and thanksgiving which could be used in the simple services of those primitive days.

Looking back to the opening Christian centuries, our attention is at once attracted to a small group of hymns which are in a class by themselves. Like commanding peaks, they tower above their fellows, bathed in the glory of the upper sky. They have this in common: they are anonymous; they are in measured prose rather than definite meter; they are a growth from a simple germ to their present form; and their outstanding merit has given them a permanent place in the liturgies of the Church. The oldest of the group is the "Tersanctus" or "Thrice Holy." Before the coming of Jesus, the Song of the Seraphim as heard by Isaiah, "Holy, holy, holy is the Lord of hosts; the whole earth is full of his glory" (Isaiah 6. 3), was chanted in the Jewish temple service. No doubt it was familiar to the Master and many of his followers. It was natural that the converts from the old faith should continue to use this beautiful ascription which they had known and loved from childhood. In the slightly changed form in which it has been used through the Christian centuries it dates back possibly to 200 A.D. or even before: "Holy, Holy, Holy, Lord God of Hosts, heaven and earth are full of thy glory. Glory be to thee, O Lord Most High!"

On the first Christmas night the angels sang the original "Glory to God in the highest," and in this form it was probably used in the days of the apostles. Then as time went on it was expanded into the noble hymn that has been sung ever since. How the words sweep through the gamut of spiritual experience! One moment the jubilant outburst of "Glory be to God," the next the miserere of sin-burdened souls; and then the quiet assurance of a simple faith in the holy and gracious One on High:

"Glory be to God on high, and on earth peace, good will toward men! We praise thee, we bless thee, we worship thee, we glorify thee, we give thanks to thee for thy great glory, O Lord God, heavenly King, God the Father Almighty! O Lord, the only begotten Son Jesus Christ; O Lord God, Lamb of God, Son of the Father, that takest away the sins of the world, have mercy upon us. Thou that takest away the sins of the world, have mercy upon us. Thou that takest away the sins of the world, receive our prayer. Thou that sittest at the right hand of God the Father, have mercy upon us. For thou only art holy; thou only art the Lord. Thou only, O Christ, with the Holy Ghost, art most high in the glory of God the Father. Amen."

It is highly fitting that the "Tersanctus" and the "Gloria in Excelsis," these two hymns "begun in heaven, finished on earth," should have a place in the Holy Communion service, that innermost sanctuary of Christian worship. The "Gloria Patri," often called the "Lesser Doxology," to distinguish it from the "Gloria in Excelsis," or "Greater Doxology," also bears the marks of antiquity. The second half, "As it was in the beginning, is now, and ever shall be, world without end," was added somewhat later; but the first half, "Glory be to the Father and to the Son and to the Holy Ghost," may be traced back almost, if not quite, to the first century, when it was the favorite doxology among the Christians.

Many lovers of Christian song give the supreme place to that noble anthem, the "Te Deum Laudamus." Would that we knew who wrote it! It has often been assigned to Ambrose, the famous Bishop of Milan, who died in 397 A.D.; but while he may have helped in its later development, the germ appeared much earlier, and grew till it reached this final form somewhere between 400 and 450 A.D. Breathing the spirit of the greatest of the ancient psalms, rising to the full altitude of Christian hope and faith, it treads the high places of sacred song with a stately dignity rarely equaled and never surpassed. No wonder that the grandest cathedrals have echoed its strains, that it has been chanted at the coronation of kings and sung by victors on the field of battle. Nor in all the centuries has it ever been put to a worthier use than on that memorable day when the tidings flashed the world around that the Great War was ended, and people of many lands and of many races voiced their grateful joy in the jubilant words:

"We praise thee, O God, we acknowledge thee to be the Lord. All the earth doth worship thee, the Father everlasting. To thee all Angels cry aloud, the heavens and all the Powers therein. To thee Cherubim and Seraphim continually do cry,

Holy, Holy, Holy, Lord God of Sabaoth
Heaven and earth are full of the majesty of thy Glory.
The glorious company of the Apostles praise thee.
The goodly fellowship of the Prophets praise thee.
The noble army of Martyrs praise thee.
The holy Church throughout all the world doth
    acknowledge thee. . . .
Day by day we magnify thee;
And we worship thy Name ever, world without end."

It is an interesting fact that in the early Christian centuries, explain it as we may, the minor key was rarely sounded. The disciples may have been under cruel persecution, facing torture, dungeon, martyrdom, but they were joyous. The art of those days depicted Jesus as a sunnyfaced young man with a rescued sheep on his shoulder. We search in vain the monuments of the first four centuries for a single instance of the crucifixion. It was the same with the hymns. Suffering, death, retribution are never mentioned; everywhere the note of praise, of exultant triumph.

The great hymns of which we have been speaking, beginning with the Advent group, belong to the Church Universal; they rise high above sectarian limits; the breath of heaven is on them. Are they not a part of that blessed tie that after all "may bind our hearts in Christian love"?

II

SYRIAC AND GREEK HYMNS

WE TURN NOW to hymns of another class. While not equal to those just described, representing rather the general average of hymnody as it has come down through the centuries, they have this interest; that, as a rule, we know who wrote them, and also their approximate time and place. These hymns naturally fall into two main groups, according to whether they appeared in the East from Syrian or Greek Christians, or in the West in the Latin tongue. On the Mediterranean seacoast, just north of Palestine proper, lies Antioch, the capital of ancient Syria and forever famous as the place where the disciples were first called Christians. We cannot be far astray if we think of this city as the nursery of Christian song. Ignatius had been bishop there so long that he knew some of Paul's friends. Tradition relates that such was his fondness for good singing that he introduced among the Christians the responsive chanting of hymns, a custom that subsequently became widespread.

The one, however, among the Syrians with whom we are chiefly concerned is the monk Ephraem. The ancient city of Edena, in Mesopotamia, early became a Christian center. All went well till the latter part of the second century, when a teacher by the name of Bardesanes arose. He claimed to be a Christian; but he did more harm than good, for his religion was distorted by the gnostic heresy. He was a gifted man, both a poet and a musician, and in order to give wings to his views he put them in the form of hymns, which in time were set to popular tunes. The novelty appealed to the people. Even the children learned the hymns and went about singing them at work and at play.

Bardesanes had been dead many years, but the mischief

was still going on when Ephraem the Syrian came to Edena.
He was a distinguished church leader, and he viewed with
alarm the inroads that heresy had made upon the old-time
faith. He determined to attack the enemy with their own
form of weapon. He began writing orthodox hymns for
both public and private use; he adopted tunes that the
people already knew and loved, taking some of the very
ones that Bardesanes had composed. Then he organized
and personally trained choirs of young women to sing his
hymns in proper form, and they led in choruses on Sundays
and feast days. The result was that the whole city was
stirred, crowds came to the orthodox services and heresy was
driven from the field. Ephraem's writings are little known
today, but he is gratefully remembered as the gifted and
brave pioneer among churchmen in producing hymns for
public worship, and in putting the musical service on a distinctly popular basis. His example and influence passed far
beyond his own land and time.

Much more extensive than the contributions from the
Syrian Christians were those from the Greek Church. The
great anonymous hymns already mentioned were for the most
part written in the Greek tongue; but, as we have stated,
they are such a definite part of the liturgy of the Church
Universal that they fall into a class by themselves. The
hymn that has the distinction of being the oldest *versified* Christian hymn in the world, and whose *author*
we know, comes to us from Egypt. Eighteen hundred years
ago Alexandria was a center of commerce and learning. The
schools of the pagans had long been famous, and the Christians were establishing their own. One day there arrived,
perhaps from Athens, a young man by the name of Clement.
He was unusually gifted and he was restlessly seeking religious light. In his new home he found Christ, and in time
he was called to the headship of the school whose converts
from paganism were instructed in the Christian doctrines.
It was then that he wrote the work entitled "The Tutor," intended as a guide to those who were entering the Church,

at the close of which he appended two hymns, the first of which is the better known. In a literal translation it opens as follows:

> Bridle of untamed colts,
> Wing of unwandering birds,
> Sure Helm of babes,
> Shepherd of royal lambs!
> Assemble thy simple children,
> To praise holily,
> To hymn guilelessly
> With innocent mouths
> Christ, the Guide of children.

It is unlikely that this hymn would ever have become known to the Church at large, had it not been that in 1846 Henry M. Dexter, pastor of the Congregational church in Manchester, New Hampshire, made a free rendering which has been in popular use ever since:

> Shepherd of tender youth,
> Guiding in love and truth
>   Through devious ways;
> Christ our triumphant King,
> We come thy name to sing;
> Hither our children bring
>   To shout thy praise.

This ancient hymn, dating from before the year 200 A.D., gathers about it a deep and tender interest. Serious times those were; it meant something to be a Christian. "Daily," says Clement, "martyrs are burnt, beheaded, and crucified before our eyes." Presently he himself was obliged to flee from the city to save his life. All through those perilous days he was constantly thinking of his flock, so many of them, whether old or young, mere "babes in Christ," and for them he sang and prayed. How fitting that this ancient hymn should be one especially suited to children!

A close competitor of the hymn by Clement, in point of age, is the one familiarly called the "Lamplighting" or "Candlelight" hymn. As the "Gloria in Excelsis" was commonly sung in the morning, so this was used in the evening. Like its distinguished companion, it is in measured prose, and it speaks to us with peculiar charm from the very early days, before the period of stately cathedral and gorgeous ceremonial had arrived. The disciples met often, perhaps in some modest sanctuary, or in the upper room of a private home. The eventide was a favorite hour, and as the shadows fell and the lamps or candles were lighted, from happy and grateful hearts the words ascended:

> O gladsome Light
> Of the Father Immortal,
> And of the celestial,
> Sacred and blessed
> Jesus our Saviour!
>
> Now to the sunset
> Again hast thou brought us;
> And seeing the evening
> Twilight, we bless thee,
> Praise thee, adore thee.
>
> Father Omnipotent!
> Son, the Life-giver!
> Spirit, the Comforter!
> Worthy at all times
> Of worship and wonder!

At a later date this hymn became a part of the service of the Greek Church and for many centuries it has been sung at the daily vespers.

During a long period following Clement, hymns written by the Greek Christians were, for the most part, either too short-lived to leave any permanent impression, or were from theologians like Gregory of Nazianzus or Synesius, and, while valuable for devotional reading, were not adapted nor intended for use in public worship. Moreover, some of the Church Fathers had scruples against the formal use of any hymn but the psalms of David, and the heretical teachers' habit of scattering their views through the medium of song strengthened the general spirit of caution. But, as we have seen in the case of Ephraem, hymns may be effective for good as well as for ill.

In the fourth century, and still later, Arianism, which denied the deity of Christ, was the dominant heresy. It had been officially condemned and yet it flourished. In those days Constantinople was the capital of the Empire, and when Chrysostom came there as bishop he had a strange experience. He was the mightiest preacher of the age; men called him the "golden mouth." But with all his eloquence he was outwitted by the Arians. They were in the habit, on Saturdays and Sundays and great festivals, of marching through the streets after sunset, singing Arian hymns and anthems. Their influence was prodigious, and even Chrysostom was balked. Then he turned the tables. With the financial aid of the Empress Eudoxia, he organized splendid processions of the orthodox party, and they went forth carrying torches and crosses, and singing with imperial pomp the hymns of Christ. Often, gathered in the church porticoes "glowing with the processional torches," they would spend the long, quiet hours of the night in song. Not only was the enemy put to shame, but it led to a much freer use of hymns in the church services, both by day and at night.

Not till we approach the close of the seventh century do we come to the really great hymn writers of the Greek Church, and they die out within a period of two hundred years. St. Andrew of Crete was born in Damascus and later became archbishop of the island that Paul and Barnabas knew so well. At one time he drifted from the orthodox fold, but afterward returned and posterity has rewarded him by enrolling him among the saints. What concerns us, however, is the fact that he was a voluminous writer of sacred poetry. His longest production was a penitential psalm of more than two hundred and fifty stanzas. So highly has it been regarded in the Greek Church that to this day it is sung entire at the Lenten season, though the exercise consumes several hours. Many passages strike a note of such genuine sincerity that they at once appeal to us:

Whence shall my tears begin?
  What first-fruits shall I bear
Of earnest sorrow for my sin?
  Or how my woes declare?
O Thou! the merciful and gracious One,
Forgive the foul transgressions I have done.

I lie before thy door,
  O turn me not away!
Nor in my old age give me o'er
  To Satan for a prey!
But ere the end of life and term of grace,
Thou Merciful, my many sins efface!

Till recently it was supposed that Andrew of Crete was likewise the author of that challenging hymn, so worthy a favorite with the Church Militant:

Christian! dost thou see them
  On the holy ground,
How the powers of darkness
  Rage thy steps around?
Christian! up and smite them,
  Counting gain but loss;
In the strength that cometh
  By the holy Cross.

Later research shows, however, that while no doubt of Greek origin, this must be placed in the long line of anonymous hymns.

Southeast from Jerusalem, where the mountains fall away into the chasm of the Dead Sea, is the monastery of Mar Saba, founded more than fourteen hundred years ago. The whole region is one of unutterable desolation. No vestige of verdure is on the horizon; only naked rocks, fantastically weathered, blistering in the hot sunshine. On every hand fathomless gorges make the head reel; it is a weird spot. Clinging by its very eyelids to the sides of a gaunt precipice is the ancient convent. Again and again through the passing centuries it has been plundered by marauding bands, and the vault, piled high with the skulls of slain monks, is a mute witness to the tragedies that have been endured. Strange that so forbidding a spot should have been the birthplace of the noblest songs of the Greek Church. Perhaps the drear loneliness of the region helped to draw men's thoughts heavenward.

There arrived at Mar Saba one day, seeking membership in the brotherhood, a man of mature years who was destined to become the most illustrious inmate that the convent has ever known. He was already so eminent a scholar that the monks were almost afraid to receive him. We know him as St. John of Damascus, named for the ancient city where he was born. He ranks as one of the distinguished theologians of all history. And more than this; while theologians are not uncommon, John of Damascus became the supreme hymnist of the Eastern Church. His weighty tomes, so full of learning, are long since forgotten, but Christians everywhere will continue to sing his hymns while time endures. The two best known we associate with Easter.

Doctor Neale, to whose gifted pen we are indebted for the striking translations into English, quotes from a modern writer who describes a scene he witnessed at Athens: "As midnight approached, the Archbishop, with his priests, accompanied by the King and Queen, left the church, and stationed themselves on the platform, so that they were distinctly seen by the people. Everyone now remained in breathless expectation, holding their unlighted tapers in readiness when the glad moment should arrive, while the priests still continued murmuring their melancholy chant in a low half-whisper. Suddenly the single report of a cannon announced that twelve o'clock had struck, and that Easter day had begun; then the old Archbishop, elevating the Cross, exclaimed in a loud, exulting tone, 'Christus Anesti!' 'Christ is Risen!' and instantly every individual of all that host took up the cry with one spontaneous shout of indescribable joy and triumph, 'Christ is Risen! Christ is Risen!' At the same moment the oppressive darkness was succeeded by a blaze of light from thousands of tapers, which, communicating one from another, seemed to send streams of fire in all directions. Bands of music struck up their gayest strains; the roll of the

drum through the town, and further on the pealing of the
cannon, announced far and near 'these glad tidings of great
joy;' while from hill and plain, from the seashore and the
far olive grove, rocket after rocket, ascending to the clear
sky, answered back with their mute eloquence that Christ is
risen indeed. Everywhere men clasped each other's hands,
and congratulated one another, and embraced with coun-
tenances beaming with delight; and all the while, rising
above the mingling of many sounds, the aged priests were
distinctly heard chanting forth a glorious old hymn of vic·
tory." Written long ago by John of Damascus, this was
the hymn:

> The day of resurrection,
>   Earth, tell it out abroad,
> The passover of gladness,
>   The passover of God.
> From death to life eternal,
>   From earth unto the sky,
> Our Christ hath brought us over
>   With hymns of victory.
>
> Our hearts be pure from evil,
>   That we may see aright
> The Lord in rays eternal
>   Of resurrection light;
> And, listening to his accents,
>   May hear, so calm and plain,
> His own "All Hail!" and hearing,
>   May raise the victor-strain.
>
> Now let the heavens be joyful!
>   Let Earth her song begin!
> Let the round world keep triumph,
>   And all that is therein!
> Invisible and visible,
>   Their notes let all things blend,
> For Christ the Lord hath risen,
>   Our joy that hath no end.

The other Easter hymn from this same pen is equally
familiar and loved:

> Come, ye faithful, raise the strain
>   Of triumphant gladness!
> God hath brought his Israel
>   Into joy from sadness;
> Loosed from Pharaoh's bitter yoke
>   Jacob's sons and daughters;
> Led them with unmoistened foot
>   Through the Red Sea waters.

If the Eastern Church had given us nothing more than these twin victorious lyrics we should be its debtors forever.

There is another hymn of entirely different tone, generally attributed to John of Damascus, and which we may call "The Last Kiss." For centuries it has been used among the Greek Christians as a funeral hymn, and there runs through it an almost weird strain. Doctor Neale tells us that it is "sung towards the conclusion of the Funeral Office, while the friends and relations are, in turn, kissing the corpse; the priest does so last of all. Immediately afterward it is borne to the grave; the priest casts the first earth on the coffin with the words, 'The earth is the Lord's and all that therein is; the compass of the world, and they that dwell therein.'" The hymn opens as follows:

> Take the last kiss—the last forever!
>   Yet render thanks amidst your gloom;
> He, severed from his home and kindred,
>   Is passing onwards to the tomb.
> For earthly labor, earthly pleasures
>   And carnal joys, he cares no more;
> Whose are his kinsfolk and acquaintance?
>   They stand upon another shore.
> Let us say, around him pressed,
> Grant him, Lord, eternal rest!

While John was living at home in his native Damascus, his father, a man of influence as well as large and generous heart, adopted an orphan boy by the name of Cosmas. The lads grew up together. They were foster brothers, and also far more: there was from the start a spiritual kinship that knit them to one another in a friendship as sacred as it was enduring. In time both men became monks at Mar Saba

and, singularly enough, both developed exceptional talent
as hymnists. If history gives the first rank to John, Cosmas
was a close second. He was called the "Melodist," and after
he died it was said of him:

> Where perfect sweetness dwells is Cosmas gone;
> But his sweet lays to cheer the church live on.

The brothers were a spur to each other in hymn writing;
there was a holy rivalry between them, and each helped the
other in correcting his verses.

Unfortunately very little from the pen of Cosmas has
found its way into our modern hymnals. The following
lines on the Transfiguration have a limited use:

> In days of old on Sinai
>   The Lord Almighty came
> In majesty of terror,
>   In thundercloud and flame;
> On Tabor, with the glory
>   Of sunniest light for vest,
> The excellence of beauty
>   In Jesus was expressed.
> All light created paled there,
>   And did him worship meet;
> The sun itself adored him
>   And bowed before his feet;
> While Moses and Elias,
>   Upon the Holy Mount,
> The coeternal glory
>   Of Christ our God recount.

His hymn for Christmas is perhaps the finest Cosmas ever
wrote. Parts of it rehearse the ancient story with all the
beautiful simplicity of Luke himself:

> The shepherds keep their flocks by night;
> The heaven glows out with wondrous light;
> The glory of the Lord is there,
> The angel-bands their King declare;
> The watchers of the night confessed,
> "God of our Father! Thou art blessed!"

The angels ceased; and suddenly
Seraphic legions filled the sky;
"Glory to God!" they cry again,
"Peace on the earth! goodwill to men;
Christ comes!"—And they that heard confessed,
"God of our Father! Thou art blessed!"

What said the shepherds?—"Let us turn
This newborn miracle to learn."
To Bethlehem's gates their footsteps drew;
The Mother with the Child they view;
They knelt and worshiped, and confessed,
"God of our Father! Thou art blessed!"

One day there came to Mar Saba a ten-year-old boy by
the name of Stephen. How amazed the cowled inmates
must have been to see a mere child among them! And what
a place for a boy to grow up, amidst the savage nakedness
of this wild abode—no companions save the dark-visaged
monks! But he was brought there by his uncle, John of
Damascus, who believed this was the safest retreat from the
devil, the world and the flesh. For fifty-nine long years it
was the only home that Stephen knew. When the end came,
what a transition from the arid rocks of Mar Saba to the
verdant fields of Paradise! It was but natural that, like
John and Cosmas, Stephen should become a hymn writer.
The one English hymn associated with his name, and which
is such a universal favorite, is not, strictly speaking, a rendering from what he wrote. But the suggestion and the
inspiration, as well as part of the language, are from him,
so that as we read the lines we can feel the heart throb and
hear the voice of the singer of old:

Art thou weary, art thou languid,
    Art thou sore distrest?
"Come to me," saith One, "and coming,
    Be at rest!"

Hath he marks to lead me to him,
    If he be my guide?
"In his feet and hands are wound-prints,
    And his side."

To bring out the real meaning and beauty of the hymn, the questions and answers should be sung by different voices. A congregation may readily be trained to give the appropriate response.

Not far from Constantinople was the Studium, the most celebrated monastery of the Greek Church. Among its inmates at different times were a number of singers, and one in particular, Theodore of the Studium. Quite apart from his poetical gifts we admire him for his unflinching heroism. He dared to condemn the emperor to his face for gross immoralities, and more than once his strenuous convictions brought him under cruel persecution, even to the gates of death. Among his hymns was one on the Last Judgment, which reveals the somber spirit of the man of iron who wrote it. He wanted men to feel that "it is a fearful thing to fall into the hands of the living God." These stanzas will give an idea of the whole:

> That fearful Day, that Day of speechless dread,
> When thou shalt come to judge the quick and dead—
>   I shudder to foresee,
>   O God, what then shall be!
>
> The Day is near, the judgment is at hand,
> Awake, my soul, awake, and ready stand!
> Where chiefs shall go with them that filled the throne,
> Where rich and poor the same tribunal own;
>   And every thought and deed
>   Shall find its righteous meed.
>
> When thou, the nations ranged on either side,
> The righteous from the sinners shalt divide,
> Then give me to be found among thy sheep,
> Then from the goats thy trembling servant keep;
>   That I may hear the voice
>   That bids thy saints rejoice!

Needless to say, this hymn by Theodore cannot compare with "the unapproachable majesty" of the "Dies Irae." But it was written four hundred years before the latter, and, as Doctor Neale has said, during that long period "it was undoubtedly the grandest Judgment-hymn of the Church."

Belonging to this same golden age of Greek hymnody we are studying is a poet who wrote more than a hundred hymns that have come down to us, and yet of whose life we know practically nothing. His name was Anatolius, and there is a vague surmise that he was a pupil of the Theodore already mentioned. There are usually ascribed to him those beautiful lines on Christ stilling the tempest, which Doctor Neale has so felicitously rendered into English, and which are so highly regarded in congregational song and especially in anthems:

> Fierce was the wild billow,
>   Dark was the night;
> Oars labored heavily,
>   Foam glimmered white;
> Trembled the mariner,
>   Peril was nigh;
> Then said the God of God,
>   "Peace! It is I."
>
> Ridge of mountain-wave,
>   Lower thy crest!
> Wail of Euroclydon,
>   Be thou at rest!
> Sorrow can never be,
>   Darkness must fly,
> When saith the Light of Light,
>   "Peace! It is I!"
>
> Jesus, Deliverer,
>   Come thou to me;
> Soothe thou my voyaging
>   Over life's sea;
> Thou, when the storm of death
>   Roars, sweeping by,
> Whisper, O Truth of Truth,
>   "Peace! It is I."

Happily the worth of a hymn is not measured by our knowledge of the author, else our collection would be robbed of some of our choicest treasures. From amid the shadows of the seventh or eighth century comes that exquisite evening hymn:

The day is past and over;
  All thanks, O Lord, to thee;
I pray thee that offenseless
  The homes of dark may be.
O Jesus, keep me in thy sight,
And save me through the coming night.

Who wrote it is quite uncertain, but we know that it was soon taken in the Service Book of the Greek Church, and at the vesper hour its words rose in sonorous chant as the priests moved in solemn procession down the dimly-lighted aisles. Through all the long centuries this old hymn has never lost its beauty, nor was it ever more of a favorite than now.

III

LATIN HYMNS

WHEN WE TURN from the hymns of the East to those of the West we are conscious of a difference. Christian hymnody was born among the Syrians and the Greeks; and Italy, Spain, Gaul and other parts of the Empire, to which it afterward came, were deeply indebted to the Eastern Church. We also gladly recognize the rare beauty in form and thought and the clear note of spiritual sincerity in the best of the Eastern hymns, some of which are unsurpassed. And yet, when we look at the whole and make comparisons from the days of Ambrose down through the centuries, we see at once that the West has the advantage. Just as religious life in general among the Western peoples showed a fullness and virility superior to that of the East, so it was with sacred song. It is true in quantity, but chiefly in quality, as a rule. The Western hymn reveals a devotional tone, a spiritual passion and often a strain of mysticism, that lift it out of the ordinary and greatly enrich its character.

Hilary, who in the middle of the fourth century was bishop of the ancient city of Poitiers in Gaul, is the first Latin hymnist. But it is not so much *what* he wrote, as *why* he wrote, that interests us. The Arian heresy was in all its glory, so that even the emperor had been seduced by it. Hilary was one of its bitterest foes; he came to be known as "the hammer of the Arians." So militant was he that he publicly denounced the emperor as Antichrist, and at once he was banished to Phrygia in Asia Minor. But Arianism was there also, and for the first time Hilary saw people in church and out, singing their religion. Presently, when his exile ended, he came home with a glowing idea, like Ephraem and Chrysostom, of the effective use that might be made of Christian song in combating false doctrine. At once he set about composing hymns, and he actually prepared a hymn-book for the congregations of his diocese, which, unfortunately, has been lost. Strange that, both East and West, heresy had so much to do with the larger use of song in Christian worship.

Presently, however, the same Province of Gaul gave to the world a far greater than Hilary. Ambrose is one of the most imposing figures in the history of the Church. Probably no one ever lived, not excepting even Gregory the Great, who left a deeper impress on the musical side of public worship. He was born about the year 340 A.D., the son of a Roman nobleman. Tradition tells how one day, when the baby was asleep in the courtyard, a swarm of bees flew about his head. The alarmed nurse started to drive them away, but the father checked her. It was a good omen, said he, and betokened coming greatness for the child. Ambrose entered public life and when a young man of thirty he was made prefect of Upper Italy, with his home at Milan, the Athens of the West.

Not long after this, the Bishop of Milan died. He belonged to the Arian party, and at once a crisis arose. The feeling between the orthodox Christians and the Arians was intensely bitter. Fearing an outbreak and possible bloodshed, the prefect went to the church, and himself presided over the election of a new bishop. His calm, dignified and gracious manner at once had a quieting effect. Instinctively the people felt that a master was in control. Suddenly, in a momentary pause, a child's voice, rang out, "Ambrose for bishop!" An instant's startled hush, and then the whole crowd took up the cry, "Ambrose for bishop!" Absurd idea!—a man of spotless character and a professing Christian, but a mere layman and not even baptised. With tears he protested, "I am not fit; I am a sinful man!" "Thy sins be upon us," the multitude cried. The voice of the child was the voice of God, and Ambrose became bishop.

Henceforward timidity and hesitation were forever gone;

he was indeed the master. At once he set about improving
the services in his own cathedral, especially the music and
the hymns. The times were favorable. For more than three
hundred years the Eastern Church had led the way in the
use of song in public worship. In the meanwhile great
changes were taking place in the West. The Christians
ceased to be a despised and persecuted people. They rapidly grew in numbers and wealth and in social and political
prestige. When Constantine accepted the faith, early in the
fourth century, Christianity was at once lifted to a dominant
place in the empire. Finer churches were now demanded
and a more elaborate ritual. Ambrose was quick to discern
the need of the hour; he determined to have the best in worship, and to place the Church of Christ in a position to
command the highest respect and reverence.

From the very birth of the Church the disciples sang
psalms and hymns, but we are completely in the dark as to
the melodies used. All records of Hebrew music have long
since disappeared, and no tunes from the early Christian
centuries have been preserved. Antiphonal chanting was
an ancient custom with the Jews, and naturally it passed
over among the Christians. But then, and for a long time
to come, religious, as well as secular, music must have been
closely limited in its scope. The day had not yet dawned
in musical progress when harmony, as we understand it, was
known and practiced, and the music was always made subordinate to the words. With sporadic exceptions, it had
been the custom in the West among persons holding minor
clerical positions to render the psalms and hymns in a "semi-
musical recitation," "more speaking than singing."

Among the improvements made by Ambrose was the intro-
duction of four chant tunes which seem to have been founded
on the ancient Greek music. The whole manner of singing
became more refined and artistic, and the congregation as
well as the choir participated in it. The changes and addi-
tions then made greatly enriched public worship. While we
are not to suppose that in wealth of musical expression the

service of the fourth century could compare with that of the
twentieth, the reforms introduced by Ambrose were so far-
reaching that they mark an epoch in the growth of Christian
worship.   The music arranged by him for the Milan Cathedral was afterward adopted in Rome, and quite generally
in the West, and, in a modified form, it is believed by some
still to continue in the Western Churches.

At the very time that Ambrose was putting through this
reform movement, there occurred his famous conflict with
Justina, the empress mother.   The Arians had been thwarted
but not conquered, and now they clamored that a church be
turned over to them for their use.   Justina, herself an Arian,
supported the demand, but Ambrose boldly refused.   They
might banish, they might slay him; yield he would not.
Soldiers were sent to seize the church, but they found a
bishop and a throng of Christians in possession.   The struggle became a veritable siege, and the watchers remained on
guard day and night.   Then it was, as Augustine tells us,
"lest the people should grow weary and faint through their
sorrows," that the idea occurred to Ambrose to hearten them
by teaching them to sing.   He was simply following the
custom of the Eastern Church, which Hilary had started to
introduce in the West.   He used some of the older hymns
and wrote some of his own, and he also composed suitable
tunes.   Needless to say, he came off victor against Justina,
and incidentally emphatic aid was given in popularizing
sacred song.

Not more than ten or twelve hymns have been preserved
which we feel safe in attributing to Ambrose.   But if his
own production was small, we know that he founded a school
of hymn writers which "held possession of the Church of
the whole of Europe for some 1200 years" (Professor F. M.
Bird).   Probably the best of his own hymns is the one for
Christmas:

> Come, thou Redeemer of the earth,
> Come, testify thy Virgin Birth;
> All lands admire, all times applaud;
> Such is the birth that fits a God.

> Thy cradle here shall glitter bright,
> And darkness breathe a newer light,
> Where endless faith shall shine serene,
> And twilight never intervene.

Even more widely sung is the Morning Hymn:

> O Splendor of God's glory bright,
> From light eternal bringeth light,
> Thou Light of light, light's living Spring,
> True Day, all days illumining.
>
> Come, very Sun of heaven's love,
> In lasting radiance from above,
> And pour the Holy Spirit's ray
> On all we think or do today.
>
> O joyful be the passing day
> With thoughts as pure as morning ray,
> With faith like noontide shining bright,
> Our souls unshadowed by the night.

Ambrose wrote also an Evening Hymn, which, in addition to its intrinsic merit, bears a peculiarly tender association.

One Sunday there was present at the service, which Ambrose was conducting, a young man, Augustine by name, destined to become the greatest of all the Church Fathers. Born in North Africa, reared in the Christian faith by Monica, one of the saintliest of mothers, he finally grew restless and left home. He would go where no one could find him. To Italy and to far-off Milan he came, and there he fell into sin. He heard everyone talking of Ambrose, the mighty preacher, and out of curiosity he went to hear him. He was impressed, but no more, and every day he sank deeper. He thought he was safe, a stranger in a strange land. But the mother's heart yearned for him, and she followed him all the way to Milan. With bitter weeping she poured out her grief before Ambrose. "Wait," said he, "wait patiently; the child of these tears cannot perish;" and presently her prayers were answered in the remarkable conversion of her son.

Augustine and Monica were twin souls, so deep was their mutual love. When the mother died the son was heart-broken, and on the night after the funeral he went to his room stricken with sorrow. "As I lay alone upon my bed," he says, "there came into my mind those true verses of Ambrose, 'for Thou art

> Maker of all things! God most high!
> Great Ruler of the starry sky!
> Robing the day in beauteous light,
> In sweet repose the quiet night;
> That sleep may our tired limbs restore,
> And fit for toil and use once more,
> May gently soothe the careworn breast,
> And lull our anxious griefs to rest.' "

No one was impressed more deeply than Augustine with the changes introduced by Ambrose. He wrote in his Confessions, addressing himself to God, but in reference to the church service, "How I wept at Thy hymns and canticles, touched to the quick by the voice of Thy melodious Church. Those voices flowed into my ears, and the truth distilled into my heart, and thence there streamed forth a devout emotion, and my tears ran down, and happy was I therein."

In the simple worship of the primitive Christians there was a large measure of freedom, especially in song. But as ritualism grew, the tendency increased for church officials to take over all but the subordinate parts. It was inevitable and, in the earlier stages at least, it was due less to an arbitrary desire of the clergy than to the fact that the laymen as a whole were ignorant of the arts of poetry and music. Ambrose went as far as possible in the direction of popular song, but the demand of liturgic music for a trained choir became imperative, and the time arrived when the part taken by the laity was restricted to brief responses. And yet the people were by no means silenced. If limited in the liturgical services, the occasions were numerous when there was perfect freedom. "As ceremonies multiplied and festivals increased in number, hymnody was stimulated, and lyric song for private and social edification, for the hours of prayer and for use in processions, pilgrimages, dedications and other occasional celebrations, were rapidly produced." (Edward Dickinson, "Music in the History of the Western Church," page 56.)

While Ambrose was improving church music in Italy, Prudentius was writing hymns in Spain. He was a layman, a lawyer by profession, and after years spent in public stations as judge and governor, when well past middle life and wearied of all that the world could give him, he determined to spend the rest of his days in the service of Christ and the Church. He wrote much and he also wrote well, if we may judge from the extraordinary popularity of his poetry, especially in the Middle Ages. A few of his hymns are in use today, including this beautiful Christmas hymn:

> Of the Father's love begotten
>   Ere the world began to be,
> He is Alpha and Omega,
>   He the source and ending he
> Of the things that are, that have been,
>   And that future years shall see,
>   Evermore and evermore.
>
> This is he whom seers in old-time
>   Chanted of with one accord,
> Whom the voices of the prophets
>   Promised in their faithful word;
> Now he shines, the long-expected;
>   Let creation praise its Lord,
>   Evermore and evermore.
>
> O ye heights of heaven, adore him;
>   Angel-hosts, his praises sing;
> All dominions, bow before him,
>   And extol our God and King;
> Let no tongue on earth be silent,
>   Every voice in concert ring,
>   Evermore and evermore.

The best that Prudentius gave the Church, in our modern judgment, was his burial hymn. It is better known in Ger-

many than in either England or America. Mrs. Charles,
from whose beautiful rendering into English we quote a few
lines, tells us that "after lying comparatively dormant from
the fourth century to the sixteenth, it awoke to life as the
favorite funeral hymn of the Protestants of Germany."

> Ah! hush now your mournful complainings,
>   Nor, mothers, your sweet babes deplore;
> This death we so shrink from but cometh
>   The ruin of life to restore.
>
> Who now would the sculptor's rich marble,
>   Or beautiful sepulchres crave?
> We lay them but here in their slumber;
>   This earth is a couch, not a grave.
>
> For quickly the day is approaching,
>   When life through these cold limbs shall flow,
> And the dwelling restored to its inmate,
>   With the old animation shall glow.
>
> The seed, which we sow in its weakness,
>   In the spring shall rise green from the earth;
> And the dead, we thus mournfully bury,
>   In God's springtime again shall shine forth.

On a spring day in the year 1416, Jerome of Bohemia was condemned to be burned at the stake for his
Protestant heroism. As they led him forth a paper cap
painted over with red devils was put on his head. When the
executioner wished to start the fire behind his back that he
might not see it, he said, "Come here and light the fire in
front of me. If I had been afraid of it, I should never have
come to this place." And as the flames mounted he burst
into song, "Salve, festa dies!" He knew it well and it was
a wonderful comfort to him in that trying hour. It was the
hymn that in English form we love to sing on Easter:

> "Welcome, happy morning!" age to age shall say,
> Hell today is vanquished, heaven is won today!
> Lo, the Dead is living, God for evermore!
> Him, their true Creator, all his works adore.

The hymn that we use is part of a poem on the resurrection that was written by Fortunatus, who was born more

than a hundred years after the death of Prudentius. He was
an Italian, but spent most of his life in France. Finely
educated, young, gay and romantic, gifted in song and
verse; no castle or palace where he was not welcome, as he
sang his songs and joined in the festive mirth; the "fashion-
able poet" of his day. He became intimately acquainted
with Queen Rhadegunda and it was largely her influence
that led him into the priesthood, where he advanced till
finally he became Bishop of Poitiers. The queen added to
her other good deeds by founding a convent, and to enrich
its odor of sanctity, the emperor presented to it a number of
relics, chief among them a piece of the so-called True Cross.
As under escort of the faithful, "with lighted torches and
perfumed censers," they were borne in solemn procession to
the door of the convent, there was sung the hymn that Fortunatus had written for the occasion:

> The Royal Banners forward go;
> The Cross shines forth with mystic glow;
> When he in flesh, our flesh was made,
> Our sentence bore, our ransom paid.
>
> When deep for us the spear was dyed,
> Life's torrent rushing from his side,
> To wash us in the precious flood,
> Where mingled water flowed, and blood.
>
> Fulfilled is all that David told
> In true prophetic song of old;
> Amidst the nations, God, saith he,
> Hath reigned and triumphed from the Tree.
>
> On whose dear arm, so widely flung,
> The weight of this world's ransom hung;
> The price of human kind to pay
> And spoil the spoiler of his prey!

Doctor Neale, whose translation we have used, calls this
world-famous hymn, "one of the grandest in the treasury of
the Latin Church." To this day, on appropriate occasions,
it is sung as a processional.

Passing through the market place in Rome one day, a

monk saw several youths standing bound, waiting to be sold. Their white bodies, fair faces and golden hair, attracted his attention. "Who are these slaves?" he asked the traders. "They are Angles," was the reply. "Not Angles," said the monk with a smile, "but angels, with faces so angel-like!" And his heart yearned for the time when the gospel of Jesus Christ should reach that island home in the far north. Three years later this monk became Pope Gregory the Great, and one of his first acts was to send missionaries to Britain, the land which, in return, in an age to come, was to give to the Church so many of her noblest hymns.

Gregory was zealous, not only for missionaries, but also for good music. Two hundred years had passed since Ambrose: the Church had grown steadily, and had reached, as never before, a commanding place in the political as well as the religious world. The reforms introduced by Ambrose had wrought untold good in the enrichment of public worship, but Gregory felt that still more was needed, that the time had come for another great forward step. He increased the number of musical modes from four to eight, thus completing the tonal system of the Church. Collecting the choicest melodies already in use and adding others, he drew up a so-called Antiphonarium, consisting of hymns, with their appropriate melodies, adapted to the principal seasons of the Church.

This book, containing the system of notation invented by Gregory, was kept chained to the altar in St. Peter's in Rome, so that if in doubt at any point, the chorister might at once refer to it. To make sure of the future, Gregory founded and endowed seminaries for the study of music, and thus a constant stream of trained singers was provided. The Gregorian chant with its solemn, almost severe, monotone was felt to be peculiarly appropriate to the majesty of divine worship. Through thirteen centuries it has held its own, and is still the leading form in nearly all Catholic churches, and has influenced Protestant song, especially in the Lutheran and Anglican communions.

Gregory had been dead scarcely seventy years when Britain, for whose conversion he had prayed and toiled so earnestly, brought forth as early fruit that scholar, poet and saint known in history as the Venerable Bede. The hymns he wrote, all of them in Latin, were few in number and are not widely used, but we honor him as the father of Christian hymnody among Englishmen. He delighted in song, and in the monastery which so long was his home he daily led the singing. Often, when all alone in his cell, he would sing hymns to the accompaniment of his Saxon harp. The old chronicle tells us that when the end drew near he said to his attendant, "Raise my head in thy hand, for it will do me good to sit facing the holy place where I was wont to pray, that sitting I may call upon my Father." And then sitting on the stone floor of his cell, singing, "Glory be to the Father and to the Son and to the Holy Ghost," he went home to God.

Theodulph, Bishop of Orleans, wrote only one hymn which has been preserved, but that hymn is so sweet and appropriate that it has been sung for more than a thousand years. It is a Palm Sunday hymn, opening with the familiar lines,

> All glory, laud and honor
> To thee, Redeemer, King,
> To whom the lips of children
> Made sweet hosannas ring.

A part of the hymn, and for many centuries regularly sung, but no longer printed in our collections, is the quaint stanza:

> Be thou, O Lord, the rider,
> And we the little ass,
> That to God's holy city
> Together we may pass.

When sung by a chorus of children this hymn is peculiarly effective. It has always been a favorite with boy choirs, and in former times was often used on Palm Sunday as a children's processional as they marched along carrying palm branches and banners.

Long centuries ago there appeared the following words as
a hymn in rhythmical prose: "In the midst of life we are in
death; of whom may we seek for succor, but of thee, O Lord,
who for our sins art justly displeased?" Tradition says the
hymn was composed in the tenth century by the poet-monk
Notker, who belonged to the monastery of St. Gall in Switzerland, and that he was moved to write after watching some
workmen, at the imminent peril of their lives, throwing a
bridge across a rocky gorge. Unhappily, the tradition is
quite uncertain, but the words have a deep and abiding interest because of their solemn use in the burial service. In
an extended form the hymn came into universal use as a
prayer in time of trouble; it was sung in sonorous chant by
the priests who accompanied armies to battle; and it has
been the model for many other hymns written in the same
vein.

Belonging to this medieval period, though three hundred
years apart, are those sublime hymns, the "Veni, Creator
Spiritus," and the "Veni, Sancte Spiritus." To say who
wrote them would be a mere guess, but they need no human
sponsor, for the Divine Spirit, of whom they sing, breathes
in every line. The first of the two can be traced back to the
close of the ninth century. For a thousand years it has been
sung in the Church of Rome on the most solemn occasions,
especially in services of ordination and consecration. It is
in the ritual of the Anglican Church and from thence it
came to the Methodist Episcopal Church. It is a moment
deeply impressive when, after the stillness of silent prayer
are heard in alternate utterances these ancient lines:

Come, Holy Ghost, our souls inspire,
And lighten with celestial fire.
Thou the anointing Spirit art,
Who dost thy sevenfold gifts impart.
Thy blesséd unction from above
Is comfort, life and fire of love.

Enable with perpetual light
The dullness of our blinded sight;

Anoint and cheer our soiléd face
With the abundance of thy grace.
Keep far our foes, give peace at home;
Where thou art Guide no ill can come.

Teach us to know the Father, Son,
And thee of both to be but One;
That through the ages all along,
This may be our endless song:
Praise to thy eternal merit,
Father, Son, and Holy Spirit.

The "Veni, Sancte Spiritus" has been called the "loveliest" in the whole circle of Latin songs; certainly it ranks very high. In recent years it has generally been ascribed to King Robert II of France, that devout and guileless ruler who was more of a monk than a statesman, and whose reign, in spite of its noble charity, was one of such tragic sorrow. He loved music and poetry, and, arrayed in royal garments, he used to go to the Church of St. Denis, where he was afterward buried, and sing with the monks, himself acting as leader. We should like to think of him as the author of the "Veni, Sancte Spiritus," but clear evidence shows that this hymn did not appear till the 13th century, two hundred years after Robert's death. As in so many other cases, we must write after it, "Anonymous." We owe to Ray Palmer the beautiful rendering into English which is so widely used:

Come, Holy Ghost, in love,
Shed on us from above
    Thine own bright ray;
Divinely good thou art;
Thy sacred gifts impart,
To gladden each sad heart;
    O come today!

There is little dissent from Doctor Schaff's estimate that in the whole range of medieval hymns "the 'Dies Irae' is the grandest, the 'Stabat Mater' the most pathetic, and the 'Jesu, Dulcis Memoria' (Jesus, the very thought of thee) the sweetest and most evangelical."

This last is a poem of two hundred lines, and is fittingly

known as the "Joyful Rhythm on the Name of Jesus." It
is quite evident that the author had caught a vision of Jesus,
and that to his enraptured thought the very Name had become clothed with surpassing beauty. For centuries parts of
the poem have been sung in the original Latin or in translation. It has given us some of our loveliest hymns. We have
only to cite the lines:

> Jesus, the very thought of thee
>   With sweetness fills the breast;
> But sweeter far thy face to see,
>   And in thy presence rest;

or these:

> Jesus, thou joy of loving hearts,
>   Thou Fount of life, thou Light of men,
> From the best bliss that earth imparts
>   We turn unfilled to thee again.

The poem from which these hymns come is so indissolubly
linked with the name of Bernard of Clairvaux—"the holiest
monk that ever lived," Luther called him—that we are
loath to assign it to another. But a manuscript has come to
light, written nearly a hundred years before Bernard was
born, and in it is this very poem. It seems to be the work
of a Benedictine Abbess, but as for any details we have
none. Since the Mother of our Lord sang her Magnificat,
this is the first time in the annals of Christian hymnody that
we hear the voice of a woman, and what rare qualities of
mind and soul she must have had!

There is another well-loved hymn which is ascribed to
Bernard of Clairvaux, and which we will venture to believe
was actually written by him, the one beginning, "O sacred
Head now wounded." It is taken from a poem of three hundred and fifty lines in all, which is broken into seven sections
of fifty lines each. The sections are prayers supposed to be
addressed by an adoring spectator to seven parts of the
Body of the crucified Redeemer as he hangs on the Cross;
to the Feet, Knees, Hands, Side, Breast, Heart and Face.
From this last prayer our hymn comes. It is additionally

interesting to remember that the Latin was first rendered into German by Dr. Paul Gerhardt, the eminent seventeenth century hymnist, and that the German hymn in turn was translated into English in 1830 by the American, Dr. J. W. Alexander. As Doctor Schaff has said, it "has shown an imperishable vitality . . . proclaiming in three tongues, and in the name of three Confessions—the Catholic, the Lutheran, and the Reformed—with equal effect, the dying love of our Saviour and our boundless indebtedness to him."

> O sacred Head, now wounded,
>   With grief and shame weighed down;
> Now scornfully surrounded
>   With thorns, thine only crown;
> O sacred Head, what glory,
>   What bliss till now was thine!
> Yet, though despised and gory,
>   I joy to call thee mine.

Bernard was one of the extraordinary characters of his own age and of all ages. As a young monk of only twenty-four he led a company of fellow monks to a desolate region in northern France, a wild valley infested by robbers, and there he planted a monastery. Under his magic touch all was transformed; the name itself was changed from Valley of Wormwood to Clear Valley (Clairvaux). His influence became Europe-wide; kings, emperor, pope, all bowed to his inspired guidance. His missionaries went everywhere and founded no less than one hundred and sixty monasteries. No wonder that after his death men spoke of him as "the last of the apostles."

It is a singular fact that two Bernards, both of them monks, lived in France at the same time, and that both names are associated with some of our greatest hymns. Concerning the monk of Clairvaux we have full information; of the personal history of Bernard of Cluny we know extremely little. The most we are sure of is summed up in the bare statement that he was born of English parents on French soil, and that he spent most of his life in the monastery at Cluny. The two monasteries were in striking contrast. Clairvaux belonged to the Order of Cistercians, which had the severest monastic discipline of the age. The brethren rejoiced in poverty; they toiled early and late, and were thankful even when reduced to a meal of brackleaves. Cluny, on the other hand, had reached a height of material splendor never before approached in the history of the Church. It possessed enormous wealth; its sanctuary was one of the most magnificent in Christendom; its monks lived in luxury, and its abbott reigned like a prince. But all was not peaceful.

There was at least one brother whose soul was troubled. To him all the worldly comfort and display was a hollow mockery; how utterly out of keeping with the life and teaching of the lowly Nazarene! He felt, as did Bernard of Clairvaux, when he exclaimed; "O that I might, before dying, see the Church of God led back to the ideal of his early days. Then the net was cast, not to catch gold and silver, but to save souls. The perilous times are not impending. They are here. Violence prevails on the earth." Open remonstrance was useless, and so the monk of Cluny poured out his feelings in verse. Day after day, through years of brooding in the quiet of his cell, he wrote his poem of three thousand lines, "On Contempt of the World." It is a bitter satire, sad and gloomy, on the awful corruptions of the age, everywhere, whether within monastic walls or in the world at large. The enormity of sin, the horrors of hell, the awe-inspiring glory of heaven—all come before him. We hear him say:

> The world is very evil,
>   The times are waxing late;
> Be sober and keep vigil,
>   The Judge is at the gate;
> The Judge that comes in mercy,
>   The Judge that comes with might,
> To terminate the evil,
>   To diadem the right.

But all was not dark. He caught a vision of things celestial, as seen by John of Patmos when he wrote:

> Jerusalem the golden,
>   With milk and honey blest,
> Beneath thy contemplation
>   Sink heart and soul oppressed;
> I know not, Oh, I know not
>   What social joys are there;
> What radiancy of glory,
>   What light beyond compare.
>
> For thee, O dear, dear country,
>   Mine eyes their vigils keep;
> For very love, beholding
>   Thy happy name, they weep.
> The mention of thy glory
>   Is unction to the breast,
> And medicine in sickness,
>   And love, and life, and rest.

No hymns on heaven are so dear to the Church as those from the heart of the monk of Cluny.

A whole volume might be filled with the story of the "Dies Irae,"—"the acknowledged masterpiece of Latin Church poetry and the greatest judgment hymn of all ages." It was written about the year 1250 by the Italian monk, Thomas of Celano, a town in the Kingdom of Naples. This is his only hymn of any account, but it is ample to establish his enduring fame. In solemn and stately language he pictures the Last Judgment with its mingled glory and terror, the sounding of the Archangel's trumpet, the rising from the dead, the gathering before the throne of the Divine Majesty, the award of eternal bliss and eternal woe.

The poem has laid an amazing hold upon the world. There are more than two hundred and fifty translations into German and English, several times as many as of any other hymn. It finds its most appropriate place when sung in the service for the dead; and yet, though written primarily for private devotion, and never intended for general singing, it is directly or indirectly represented in nearly every church hymnal. It has made a profound impression on music and literature. We have only to recall Mozart's use of it in his

"Requiem." It so wrought upon him that it actually hastened his death. Goethe was very fond of it, and with what dramatic effect he brings it into the cathedral scene in "Faust," where the conscience-stricken Margaret cries out in terror as the organ suddenly begins to play, and she hears in sonorous chant,

> Dies irae, dies illa,
> Solvet seclum in favilla!

This poem fascinated Sir Walter Scott. He murmured its words as he lay in the delirium of his closing hours. It inspired that condensed version in the "Lay of the Last Minstrel," which Gladstone pronounced the sublimest lines Scott ever wrote:

> The day of wrath, that dreadful day,
> When heaven and earth shall pass away,
> What power shall be the sinner's stay?
> How shall he meet that dreadful day?
> When, shriveling like a parchéd scroll
> The flaming heavens together roll;
> When louder yet and yet more dread,
> Swells the high trump that wakes the dead,
> Oh, on that day, that wrathful day
> When man to judgment wakes from clay,
> Be thou the trembling sinner's stay,
> Though heaven and earth shall pass away.

Samuel Johnson was very fond of the "Dies Irae," but he could never read without bursting into tears the stanza, beginning,

> Quaerens me sedisti lassus.
> Wearily for me thou soughtest,
> On the Cross my soul thou boughtest,
> Lose not all for which thou wroughtest.

No translation can possibly do justice to the sublime grandeur of the original, but this one by Dr. William J. Irons is on the whole the most popular. We give it in part:

> Day of wrath! O day of mourning!
> See! once more the cross returning,
> Heaven and earth in ashes burning!

> O what fear man's bosom rendeth,
> When from heaven the Judge descendeth,
> On whose sentence all dependeth!
>
> Wondrous sound the trumpet flingeth,
> Through earth's sepulchers it ringeth,
> All before the throne it bringeth!
>
> Death is struck, and nature quaking,
> All creation is awaking,
> To its Judge an answer making!
>
> What shall I, frail man, be pleading?
> Who for me be interceding,
> When the just are mercy needing?
>
> Righteous Judge of retribution,
> Grant thy gift of absolution,
> Ere that reckoning-day's conclusion!

On a somewhat lower level than the incomparable "Dies Irae," but with points of similarity, is that other great hymn, the "Stabat Mater." It was written at about the same time as the "Dies Irae," and likewise by an Italian, Jacopone, a lay brother in the Order of St. Francis. By common consent, it is the most pathetic hymn of the Middle Ages, indeed, of any age. While its effusive references to the Virgin Mary militate against its free use in Protestant circles, the exquisite beauty of its language and the tender pathos running through it make an irresistible appeal to human hearts. The poem is based on the words in John's Gospel, "There stood by the cross of Jesus his mother," and then is depicted the grief of Mary as she beheld her suffering and dying Son. It opens with the lines:

> At the Cross her station keeping,
> Stood the mournful mother weeping,
>   Close to Jesus to the last;
> Through her heart, his sorrow sharing,
> All his bitter anguish bearing,
>   Now at length the sword had passed.

It is a beautiful thought that the words of this poem, used as the libretto, are forever embalmed in music by Palestrina, Haydn, Rossini and other eminent composers.

IV

GERMAN HYMNS

A S THE LONG medieval period rolled on, clear signs began to appear that gradually the old order was passing out and a new age was at hand. Nowhere would the change be more noticeable than in the mode and spirit in which men would worship God. For nearly a thousand years laymen had taken almost no part in church song; congregational singing was unknown. Ambrose had felt its value, and the type of music which he introduced in Milan, and which came to be known as Ambrosian, was adapted to congregational use. But difficulties arose. Church services were always in the Latin tongue, and as time went on and Christianity spread to various lands, the worshipers who understood Latin became fewer and fewer. And moreover, with the growth of form and ceremony, there was the constant trend toward stricter liturgical usage, which meant thrusting the laity farther into the background.

The trend became firmly settled with the coming of the Gregorian chant. Here was a form of music with less melody and rhythm and so difficult to acquire that it demanded highly trained singers. This, indeed, was what Gregory had in mind when he introduced it. Henceforth the musical service was to be exclusively in the hands of the clergy. A famous school was founded in Rome. The scholars were received when they were boys, and they were given years of most careful training, for they were expected to devote their life to church song. There used to be shown the sofa where Gregory reclined while personally examining the scholars. From Rome trained singers went all over Western Europe; far back in the reign of King Ethelbert forty of them carried the Gregorian chant to Britain. The Emperor Charlemagne, himself an enthusiastic lover of music, gave the movement his eager sanction by planting schools in various centers. The pioneer teachers had their trials, as one of them, toiling among the tribesmen of Germany, despairingly complained, "These gigantic bodies, whose voices roar like thunder, cannot imitate our sweet tones, for their barbarous and ever-thirsty throats can only produce sounds as harsh as those of a loaded wagon passing over a rough road." Could he have foreseen what masters of the art that land would one day produce!

Now without doubt the Gregorian service had its advantages, but it gave small place to the layman. Long before this, the Greek ejaculation, "Kyrie Eleison" and "Christe Eleison" ("Lord, have mercy!" and "Christ, have mercy!"), which from early days had been familiar to the Eastern Christians, were brought into the Western Church and provided a popular response. The Germans in particular, who were always a song-loving people, became very fond of them, and rolled them out with unbounded fervor, especially at festivals and on other great occasions. But finally they degenerated into a noisy jargon when they were repeated hundreds of times in succession, and were abbreviated to such meaningless forms as "Kyrielle" and "Kerleis," and "Kles." Yet even so they possessed a real value in being the only share that the people had in the service; and, far more, in furnishing the seed of the wonderful German hymnody of later centuries. Those bare responses were presently lengthened into brief poems called "Leichan," which were the earliest German hymns to be sung by the people. While never used in the service of the Mass, they were allowed on various popular occasions. The first of them dates back a thousand years, and refers to St. Peter:

> Our dear Lord of grace hath given
> To St. Peter power in heaven,
> That we may uphold alway
> All who hope in him, and say
>   Kyrie eleison!
>   Christe eleison!

Let us to God's servant pray,
All, with loudest voice today,
That our souls which else were lost
May dwell among the heavenly host:
  Kyrie eleison!
  Christe eleison!

At a later time came the Minnesingers, those lyric poets of Germany, who glorified love and beauty, and whose songs, often touching the deeper emotions of heart and soul, were in high repute all over the land. Then we find the Flagellanti, so-called because they preached and practiced self-scourging; strange people, both men and women, who were especially active in the middle of the fourteenth century when the Black Death was terrifying Europe. They wandered from town to town, their half-naked bodies streaked with blood, chanting weird hymns and in frenzied passion summoning the multitudes to repentance. Incidentally, in these ways the people were being accustomed to singing in their native tongue. Of still greater influence in the beginning of German hymnody were the Mystics; those earnest souls, who in an age of spiritual leanness never lost their communion with God. Chief among them was John Tauler, Dominican monk and mighty preacher, holding to his task even while the Black Death was raging. In sermon and in verse he taught the Word. We hear him singing:

O Jesus Christ, most Good, most Fair,
More fragrant than May's flowery air,
Who thee within his soul doth bear
  True cause for joy hath won!
But would one have thee in his heart
From all self-will he must depart,
God's bidding only, whom thou art,
  Must evermore be done.
Where Jesus then doth truly dwell,
His presence doth all tumults quell,
And transient cares of earth dispel
  Like mists before the sun.

From this same pen we have a Christmas carol, written in

the style of the German folk song. With its quaint symbolism it soon became a favorite:

> A ship comes sailing onwards
>> With a precious freight on board;
> It bears the only Son of God,
>> It bears th' Eternal Word.
>
> A precious freight it brings us,
>> Glides gently on, yet fast;
> Its sails are filled with Holy Love,
>> The Spirit is its mast.
>
> And now it casteth anchor,
>> The ship hath touched the land;
> God's Word hath taken flesh, the Son
>> Among us men doth stand.
>
> At Bethlehem, in the manger,
>> He lies, a babe of days;
> For us, he gives himself to death,
>> O give him thanks and praise.
>
> Whoe'er would hope in gladness
>> To kiss the Holy Child,
> Must suffer many a pain and woe,
>> Patient like him and mild;
>
> Must die with him to evil
>> And rise to righteousness,
> That so with Christ he too may share
>> Eternal life and bliss.

Henry of Laofenburg, who was a monk in Strasburg in the fifteenth century and a prolific writer of sacred verse, among other poems, has left us this lovely Cradle Song:

> Ah Jesus Christ, my Lord most dear,
> As thou wast once an infant here,
> So give this little child, I pray,
> Thy grace and blessing day by day;
>> Ah Jesus, Lord Divine,
>> Guard me this babe of mine!
>
> Now sleep, O sleep, my little child,
> Jesus will be thy playmate mild;
> Sweet dreams he sendeth thee, I trow,
> That full of goodness thou may'st grow;
>> Ah Jesus, Lord Divine,
>> Guard me this babe of mine!

So he, who hath all love and might,
Bids thee good morrow and good night.
Blest in his name thou daily art,
My child, thou darling of my heart;
　　Ah Jesus, Lord Divine,
　　Guard me this babe of mine!

While the later Middle Ages, especially among the Germans, saw an ever increasing number of songs and hymns, many of them of rare beauty and value, their use remained strictly limited. Congregational singing was still unknown. It was with the Bohemian Brethren, followers of John Huss, that the barriers were first definitely broken down. Huss died at the stake in 1415; but his spirit and teaching lived on. He believed the people ought to share in church song, and he, and his disciples after him, wrote many hymns which were used in their religious gatherings. But they were of temporary value. Huss once said, "We preach the Gospel not only from the pulpit, but even our hymns are homilies."

This was both their strength and their weakness. For the most part they were sermons in verse, valuable in teaching, but without the lyrical quality which made them singable. For this reason they were eventually discarded for something better. But what Huss and his followers did of lasting worth was as pioneers in congregational song. The collection sent out by the Bohemian Brethren in 1504 was the first real hymn book that ever appeared for the use of the congregation. Then the way was being prepared for that wonderful lyrical outburst which glorified the new age in divine worship that was now at hand.

In the city of Magdeburg there hangs a painting which tells a story of pathetic interest. A ship, representing the Church, is sailing heavenward. On board, safe and happy, overshadowed by the Holy Ghost, are pope, cardinals, bishops, priests of every degree. In the water are the laymen, some of them drowning, others struggling to draw themselves up by ropes which in pity have been thrown to them. This was the idea that for long centuries held men's minds. Two classes, sharply distinct—a company of the elect, forever secure, simply by virtue of their clerical connection; a host of the non-elect, in mortal peril, simply because they were laymen.

When finally this old belief was shattered, a shout of victory went up to heaven. Those were wonderful times, beyond anything the world had known since the coming of Jesus. Within a space of seventy-five years we date the invention of printing, the revival of learning, the discovery of America, and the Protestant Reformation! What a conspiracy of events! And best of all was the new freedom of the soul. The barriers between man and God were broken down; the priesthood of believers became a vital fact; the humblest disciple, without let or hindrance, might approach the Throne of Grace. No wonder there was an outburst of song; it was the natural expression of a great joy. This song movement, started with the Germans, entered neighboring lands, and passed over to England and Scotland.

While others, both before and after, were valuable contributors, Martin Luther was the real founder of congregational hymnody. He was a born lover of music. We picture him at his daily pastime, after dinner taking his lute and for a half hour singing and playing with his companions. "He who despises music," said he, "will never be my friend." He was quick to see what an enormous help to the new faith sacred song would be, especially among the music-loving Germans. Get the people to singing their religion, and the victory was half won. In giving to the nation the Bible and the hymn book in the mother tongue, Luther wrought better than he knew. In its wide and abiding influence, it was one of the benefactions of all time. Thirty-seven hymns may be traced to Luther himself. Some of them are translations of great Latin hymns that had long been in use. He had the good sense to reject nothing, whether words or music, simply because it came from the Church of Rome. He was a "purifier, not a destroyer." Several of his best hymns are psalm versions; but all that he wrote, whether strictly original or

based on the Latin or Hebrew, was baptized in the spirit of
the new age.

We have only to think of that lyric, Luther's greatest,
rising like a lordly peak in the range of Christian hymnody,
and whose opening line is cut in the reformer's tomb at
Wittenberg, "Ein feste Burg ist unser Gott." It was suggested by the 46th Psalm, "God is our refuge and strength,"
and appeared first in print in 1528. Nothing that Luther
ever wrote is more characteristic of the man. Its bold,
rugged lines remind us, as Carlyle says, of the "sound of
Alpine avalanches, or the first murmur of earthquakes." It
leaped into favor, and at once became the battle hymn of
the Reformation. Those were militant times, times that
tried men's souls; the pent-up issues of centuries were
finding release. Many of Luther's hymns, and especially
"Ein Feste Burg," express in every word, the feelings that
were surging through the writer's mind and heart. This
hymn defies adequate translation. The rendering found in
many hymn books is by Dr. Frederick Henry Hedge, a
Unitarian clergyman of New England, who died in 1890.
But Carlyle's version, if less smooth and singable, is more
Luther-like in its style, and we give it here:

> A safe stronghold our God is still,
>   A trusty shield and weapon;
> He'll help us clear from all the ill
>   That hath us now o'ertaken.
> The ancient prince of hell
> Hath risen with purpose fell;
> Strong mail of craft and power
> He weareth in this hour;
>   On earth is not his fellow.
>
> With force of arms we nothing can;
>   Full soon were we down-ridden;
> But for us fights the proper Man,
>   Whom God himself hath bidden.
> Ask ye, Who is this same?
> Christ Jesus is his name,
> The Lord Sabaothi Son;
> He, and no other one,
>   Shall conquer in the battle.

And were this world all devils o'er
  And watching to devour us,
We lay it not to heart so sore;
  Nothing can overpower us.
And let the prince of ill
Look grim as e'er he will,
He harms us not a whit;
For why? His doom is writ.
  A word shall quickly slay him.

God's word! for all their craft and force
  One moment will not linger;
But, spite of hell, shall have its course;
  'Tis written by his finger.
And though they take our life,
Goods, honor, children, wife;
Yet is their profit small;
These things shall vanish all;
  The city of God remaineth.

One night after Luther's death, Melancthon, who was at Weimar with some of his banished friends, in the street heard a child singing this hymn. "Sing on, my little maid," said he; "you little know what people you comfort." Its martial strains appealed to the great Swedish general, Gustavus Adolphus. His soldiers knew it by heart, and often sang it when assembled in the field. When the warlike chorus came to the lines,

Ask ye, Who is this same?
Christ Jesus is his Name,

"the whole thunder of artillery would reply with the military salute, as owning the invisible leadership of the Captain of their salvation."

Luther's first hymn was written at a time when he was passionately moved. Two young men, Augustinian monks, went over to the Reformed faith. Tried and condemned at Brussels, they were burned at the stake. They were the first martyrs to the new cause, and their death was heralded all over the land. Luther voiced his feelings in a long poem, on which are founded the familiar lines:

Fling to the heedless winds,
  Or on the waters cast,
The martyrs' ashes, watched,
  Shall gathered be at last.

And from that scattered dust,
  Around us and abroad,
Shall spring a plenteous seed
  Of witnesses for God.

*   *   *   *

Still, still, though dead, they speak,
  And trumpet-tongued, proclaim,
To many a wakening land,
  The one availing name.

Luther was a great-hearted husband and father. He was devoted to his family, and never happier than when, surrounded by his wife and six children, he led them in singing. He seems to have been peculiarly fond of little Hans, and when the child was four years old the father wrote for him a lovely Christmas song which to this day is a prime favorite with the children of Germany. It closes with the stanzas,

Ah, dearest Jesus, Holy Child,
Make thee a bed, soft, undefiled,
Within my heart, that it may be
A quiet chamber kept for thee.

My heart for very joy doth leap;
My lips no more can silence keep;
I too must sing with joyful tongue
That sweetest, ancient cradle-song,—

"Glory to God in highest heaven,
Who unto men his Son hath given!"
While angels sing with pious mirth
A glad new year to all the earth.

As rapidly as Luther's hymns appeared, they were eagerly caught up by the people. He begged his friends to help him by writing hymns after the same model, which they did. Successive collections by the score were published, and many times hymns and tunes were printed on single sheets and carried all over Germany by wandering students and peddlers. The new evangel, like a voice from the skies, coupled with the strong human touch of the hymns, appealed to both heart and soul. They were used not only in church, but an eyewitness wrote, "The artisan sings them at his work, the maid as she washes the clothes, the peasant on his furrow, the mother to the child that cries in the cradle." Cases are on record where whole towns were so moved that the people in a body went over to the new faith. No wonder that indignant Romanites declared that "Luther's songs have damned more souls than all his books and speeches."

The melodies used had much to do with the popularity of the songs. There was the same freedom and spontaneity that we find in the words. They were taken from various sources, chorales belonging to the old Latin hymns, secular melodies familiar to everyone and tunes in use among the Bohemian Brethren. Changes were made as needed to adapt them to the new hymns. Till recently, it was universally believed that Luther himself was a tune writer, but this is now positively denied. Without exception, the tunes attributed to him have been traced to earlier sources. But if he wrote no music, he showed a happy faculty in selecting good tunes, at least one of which, the one wedded to "Ein Feste Burg," is as popular today as it was four hundred years ago. Before Luther's dead body was borne to its last resting place, the weeping throng gathered in the church and sang the hymn his own hand had penned, and which has ever since been a funeral hymn among the Germans:

> Out of the depths I cry to thee,
>   Lord God, O hear my wailing!
> Thy gracious ear incline to me,
>   And make my prayer availing;
> On my misdeeds in mercy look,
> O deign to blot them from thy book,
>   Or who can stand before thee?
>
> Where'er the greatest sins abound,
>   By grace they are exceeded;
> Thy helping hand is always found
>   With aid, where aid is needed;
> Thy hand, the only hand to save,
> Will rescue Israel from the grave,
>   And pardon his transgressions.

In English-speaking lands, as a rule, we are sadly ignorant of the immense contribution that German writers have made to Protestant hymnody. For two hundred years from Luther to Watts, Germany stood practically alone as a source of Christian hymns. In the meantime, England was given to the use of psalms, and another century and more passed before English hymnists began to catch up with the Germans, either in quantity or in quality.

Within the compass of these pages reference can be made to only a few of the multitude of authors and thousands of hymns from the land of Luther; but though merely a glimpse, it may give an idea of what a treasure-house there is. During the early Reformation period appeared various writers who had the spirit of the new·age, but they were so overshadowed by Luther as to make a relatively minor impression.

Michael Weisse was born shortly before the great reformer, and, like Luther, he was first a monk. After joining the new movement, he became both preacher and poet. He wrote more than a hundred hymns that passed into the German hymn books, many of them still being sung. We think of him chiefly as the author of those fine Easter lines:

> Christ the Lord is risen again;
> Christ hath broken every chain;
> Hark, angelic voices cry,
> Singing evermore on high,
>   Alleluia!
>
> He who slumbered in the grave
> Is exalted now to save;
> Now through Christendom it rings
> That the Lamb is King of Kings.
>   Alleluia!
>
> Thou, our Paschal Lamb, indeed,
> Christ, today thy people feed;
> Take our sins and guilt away,
> That we all may sing for aye,
>   Alleluia!

In the summer and fall of 1597 a deadly pestilence swept over the little town of Unna in Westphalia. The parsonage of Philipp Nicolai, Lutheran pastor, overlooked the grave-yard, where on some days as many as thirty villagers were laid to rest. His very soul was torn with anguish by these mournful scenes, and he sought comfort and assurance by the study of God's Word and prayerful meditation on the blessed life to come. One day, after reading the parable of the Ten Virgins, with the midnight call to meet the Bride-groom, he wrote the hymn which is especially associated with his name. At once it became popular and has been sung ever since. The noble melody to which from the first it was wedded, and which has been called "the King of Chorales," is also by Nicolai. The hymn appealed so strongly to Mendelssohn that he introduced both words and music into his "St. Paul":

> Awake, awake, for night is flying;
> The watchmen on the heights are crying,
>   Awake, Jerusalem, arise!
> Midnight's solemn hour is tolling,
> His chariot wheels are nearer rolling,
>   He comes; prepare, ye virgins wise;
> Rise up; with willing feet
> Go forth, the Bridegroom meet;
>   Alleluia!
> Bear through the night your well-trimmed light,
> Speed forth to join the marriage rite.
>
> Zion hears the watchmen singing,
> Her heart with deep delight is springing,
>   At once she wakes, she hastes away;
> Forth her Bridegroom hastens glorious,
> In grace arrayed, by truth victorious;
>   Her grief is joy, her night is day;
> Hail, Worthy Champion,
> Christ, God Almighty's Son;
>   Alleluia!
> We haste along, in pomp of song,
> And gladsome join the marriage throng.

Hear thy praise, O Lord, ascending
From tongues of men and angels, blending
   With harp and lute and psaltery.
By thy pearly gates in wonder
We stand and swell the voice of thunder,
   In bursts of choral melody;
No vision ever brought,
No ear hath ever caught,
   Such bliss and joy;
We raise the song, we swell the throng,
To praise thee ages all along.

If we could bring together the prayers of a people we could write the nation's history. In a surprising degree it is likewise true of the hymns. Religious song is an outpouring of human hearts, the hopes and fears, the joys and sorrows; often the deepest thoughts and feelings are unconsciously expressed. A hymn may be the surest embodiment of the spirit of the times as well as of the writer. The very genius of the Reformation appears in "Ein Feste Burg," offspring of a bold and rugged age.

In a similar way the hymns of a century later reveal the distress of an age of war. It was the period of the Thirty Years' War, from 1618 to 1648, the darkest in the long annals of the German people. All semblance of religious truce had been swept away, and Protestantism was struggling for its very life. Through a whole generation ruffian armies swept to and fro, pillaging, burning, slaying with a pitiless ferocity that no words can describe. City and village, castles and houses without number, were laid in ashes. Nothing was too beautiful or too sacred to feel the destroyer's hand. When it was all over, the land was well-nigh a desert, more than half the people perished, four-fifths of the property gone. Two centuries later Germany was still suffering from the blows of those cruel days. And then, as if war were not enough, in the train of fire and sword came pestilence and famine, taking a deadly toll of a suffering remnant. In truth it was a darkness that could be felt; and yet in the very midst of the gloom dawned the golden age of German Hymnody.

When the Protestants were hardest pressed, the famous Swedish king, Gustavus Adolphus, "Lion of the North," came to their relief with his invincible troops. Not long after, there appeared in German a hymn of martial tone, outlined probably by the king, though actually written by some one else. On November 6, 1632, was fought the great battle of Lützen when the Swedes conquered, but their leader was slain. That morning a heavy fog enshrouded everything. At the hour of prayer the soldiers sang Luther's "Ein Feste Burg." Then, as the fog began to lift and the buglers were preparing to sound the charge, the king directed that his Battle Hymn be sung, and, accompanied by the drums and trumpets of the whole army, thousands of lusty voices pealed out the lines that are forever associated with the name of Gustavus Adolphus:

> Fear not, O little flock, the foe
> Who madly seeks your overthrow;
>   Dread not his rage and power;
> What though your courage sometimes faints?
> His seeming triumph o'er God's saints
>   Lasts but a little hour.
>
> Fear not, be strong! your cause belongs
> To him who can avenge your wrongs;
>   Leave all to him, your Lord;
> Though hidden yet from mortal eyes,
> Salvation shall for you arise;
>   He girdeth on his sword!
>
> As true as God's own promise stands,
> Not earth nor hell with all their bands
>   Against us shall prevail;
> The Lord shall mock them from his throne;
> God is with us; we are his own;
>   Our victory cannot fail!
>
> Amen, Lord Jesus, grant our prayer!
> Great Captain, now thine arm make bare;
>   Thy Church with strength defend;
> So shall thy saints and martyrs raise
> A joyful chorus to thy praise,
>   Through ages without end.

The Thirty Years' War produced no character more heroic than Martin Rinkart. The son of a humble coppersmith, he was educated for the ministry, and in time became pastor in his native town of Eilenburg. During the war he was in the very heart of the suffering area. Ruffian soldiers were billeted in his own parsonage and repeatedly he was robbed. At the height of the atrocities, when the town was crowded with refugees, a frightful pestilence broke out. Rinkart's fellow-clergymen perished and he alone was left to visit the sick and bury the dead. In a single year eight thousand fell victims, including the pastor's own wife; there were forty or fifty funerals a day. Famine speedily followed the pestilence; the starving crowd fought in the street for a dead cat or crow. As a climax, a marauding army appeared at the gates and demanded a heavy ransom. The ruined people were in utter despair, but the prayers of Rinkart touched the heart of the general and finally secured an easing of the terms. Amid all these dreadful experiences their courageous pastor never lost his faith and cheer, and as the skies began to brighten he broke forth in grateful song, giving to the world the best-known hymn of the more than two hundred he wrote. It was eagerly received and it soon became the national Te Deum of Germany. It was introduced by Mendelssohn into his "Hymn of Praise." Still sung to the original melody, it is used on thanksgiving occasions, and in Miss Wentworth's translation it is also a favorite in our English hymnals:

> Now thank we all our God
>   With hearts and hands and voices,
> Who wondrous things hath done,
>   In whom his world rejoices;
> Who, from our mothers' arms,
>   Hath blessed us on our way
> With countless gifts of love,
>   And still is ours today.
>
> O may this bounteous God
>   Through all our life be near us,
> With ever joyful hearts
>   And blessed peace to cheer us;

And keep us in his grace,
And guide us when perplexed,
And free us from all ills
In this world and the next.

In Paul Gerhardt German hymnody reached its meridian splendor. A mere boy when the Thirty Years' War broke out, he was so hindered by those troublous times, that he was in middle age before he became fully settled in his life work as a Lutheran minister. Promoted from one post to another, he was presently installed pastor of the great Church of St. Nicholas in Berlin. He was soon the favorite preacher of the city, crowds flocking to his ministry. Though escaping the tragic sufferings of Rinkart, both during the war and afterward, he passed through bitter trials. When he was at the height of success in Berlin and the idol of his parishioners, he was summarily removed from his post because he refused to surrender his liberty as a Christian minister to condemn in Calvinism what he felt was contrary to the teaching of the gospel. He retired to a small country parish, where he spent the closing years of his life. His family circle was shattered by the death of his wife and four of his five children. But his soul was never embittered, nor did he lose his serene faith in God.

Eminent as he was in the pulpit, his greatest preaching was in verse rather than in prose. He was a prince of sacred poets. In popular esteem he is outranked only by Luther. If in the later poet we miss the fire and rugged strength of the reformer, we find in Gerhardt a poetic beauty and refinement rarely seen in Luther. His poems are "songs of the heart." They were conceived and born of his own experience, but they carry a human appeal to Christians of all times and of all lands. Schiller learned them at his mother's knee and loved them through life, while to the humblest disciple they bring a similar comfort and strength. His "Hymn of Trust," written when he was passing through the deepest shadows, is unsurpassed in any tongue, and for nigh three hundred years has brought consolation to a multitude of hearts. John Wesley's noble translation in sixteen stanzas is sometimes divided into the two well-known hymns, beginning,

>Commit thou all thy griefs
>   And ways into his hands,
>To his sure trust and care
>   Who earth and heaven commands,

and

>Give to the winds thy fears;
>   Hope, and be undismayed;
>God hears thy sighs and counts thy tears;
>   God shall lift up thy head.

The tender, devotional spirit of Gerhardt is beautifully revealed in his "Love to Christ," also a translation by Wesley:

>Jesus, thy boundless love to me
>   No thought can reach, no tongue declare;
>O knit my thankful heart to thee,
>   And reign without a rival there!
>Thine wholly, thine alone, I am,
>Be thou alone my constant flame.

>*   *   *   *

>In suffering be thy love my peace;
>   In weakness be thy love my power;
>And when the storms of life shall cease,
>   O Jesus, in that solemn hour,
>In death as life be thou my guide,
>And save me, who for me hast died.

The loving, joyful trust, which appears in so many of Gerhardt's hymns, is seen in the Christmas carol:

>All my heart this night rejoices,
>   As I hear, far and near,
>Sweetest angel voices;
>"Christ is born," these choirs are singing,
>   Till the air everywhere
>Now with joy is ringing.

>Hark! a voice from yonder manger,
>   Soft and sweet, doth entreat;
>"Free from woe and danger;
>Brethren, come; from all doth grieve you
>   You are freed; all you need
>I will surely give you."

Come then, let us hasten yonder;
  Here let all, great and small,
Kneel in awe and wonder;
Love him who with love is yearning,
  Hail the Star that from far
Bright with hope is burning.

Blessèd Saviour, let me find thee;
  Keep thou me close to thee,
Cast me not behind thee;
Life of life, my heart thou stillest,
  Calm, I rest on thy breast,
All this void thou fillest.

Johann Scheffler (1624-1677) is an interesting example of
a man who was a vehement controversialist and at the same
time a mystic; who indulged in polemics even to bitterness
and also wrote deeply spiritual hymns. Brought up in the
Lutheran faith, he afterward entered the Church of Rome
and became a Jesuit. Our chief interest, however, is in the
wealth of sacred poetry that poured from his pen. The
hymn best known in English-speaking lands is the translation by John Wesley:

I thank thee, uncreated Sun,
  That thy bright beams on me have shined;
I thank thee, who hast overthrown
  My foes, and healed my wounded mind;
I thank thee whose enlivening voice
Bids my freed heart in thee rejoice.

No one ever lived who was more enraptured with Jesus
Christ than Scheffler. Love for the Master was his absorb-
ing passion and the heart and soul of his hymns. He could
sing,

Thee will I love, my strength, my tower;
  Thee will I love, my joy, my crown;
Thee will I love with all my power
  In all my works, and thee alone!
Thee will I love, till the pure fire
Fill my whole soul with chaste desire;

and again,

O Love, who formdest me to wear
　　The image of thy Godhead here;
Who soughtest me with tender care
　　Through all my wanderings wild and drear;
O Love, I give myself to thee,
Thine ever, only thine to be.

George Neumark, who enriched German hymnody at the
same period as Scheffler, suffered many trials. In his student days, while on a journey, he was attacked by bandits
and robbed of nearly all he had. Then, as he tells us,
"through a dreadful fire I came to my last farthing" (Ju-
lian; 796;1); and in later life he was afflicted with blindness. But his trust in God never failed. On one occasion,
while still a young man, he was reduced to penury through
failure to obtain employment, but he found great cheer in
the words, "Cast thy burden upon the Lord and he shall
sustain thee." When presently he was offered a tutorship,
he was so overjoyed that he wrote his "Hymn cf Consolation," the finest from his pen, and as great a favorite
abroad as in Germany. It opens with the familiar lines:

Leave God to order all thy ways,
　　And hope in him whate'er betide;
Thou'lt find him, in the evil days,
　　Thine all-sufficient strength and guide.
Who trusts in God's unchanging love
Builds on the rock that nought can move!

The melody also was composed by Neumark. It furnished
Bach with the basis for a cantata, and Mendelssohn used it
in his "St. Paul."

How many of our best hymns are an outpouring from the
crucible of personal affliction! This seems to be especially
true with those of German origin. Benjamin Schmolck, a
Lutheran pastor, born in 1672, became the most popular
hymnist of his time, and of the thousand poems from his
pen, none is better loved, certainly in American circles, than
his "Trust in God." We can feel its heart throbs in every
line. His home town nearly destroyed by fire, two of his

children taken by death, he himself, in the very crisis of his pastoral toil, stricken with paralysis which led to total blindness, he still could sing:

> My Jesus, as thou wilt;
>   O may thy will be mine!
> Into thy hand of love
>   I would my all resign.
> Through sorrow or through joy,
>   Conduct me as thine own,
> And help me still to say,
>   "My Lord, thy will be done."

In all the annals of German hymnody, no one outreaches Tersteegen in hunger for God, and few excel him in the spiritual beauty of his verse. From a child he was a devoted lover of the Master. In his early manhood there came a time of gloom, when for five years the Divine Presence seemed to be withdrawn; and then, on a day never to be forgotten, the light broke, and in rapture of heart he penned with his own blood a covenant of self-dedication to his Master. He became a mystic; soul union with God was his supreme desire. Even the simplest church forms were repugnant to him; he sought the inner light. By trade he was a weaver, but his real business was the service of his Lord. Every minute which he could take from his daily toil was spent in prayer and meditation and in teaching others.

People thought he was queer; his own kindred were ashamed of him. But as the quiet simplicity of his Christian devotion became better known, many who yearned for a closer walk with God were drawn to him from far and near. His humble abode was known as the "Pilgrim Hut," and there he counseled and wrote. He was a prolific author of sacred verse, and some of his hymns are as well known and loved in America and England as in Germany. Widely sung is the hymn suggested by the words in the Ninety-fifth Psalm, "Today if ye will hear his voice, harden not your heart":

God calling yet! shall I not hear?
Earth's pleasures shall I still hold dear?
Shall life's swift passing years all fly,
And still my soul in slumber lie?

Another favorite hymn from this same pen is that hymn
of "deepest adoration of the All-holy God," beginning,

Lo! God is here; let us adore,
    And own how dreadful is this place;
Let all within us feel his power,
    And humbly bow before his face.

But Tersteegen rose to a still greater height. Dr. Robert
Collyer tells us that he was present one day in company
with Emerson and Holmes when the subject of hymns came
up. Holmes criticized some of the hymns in common use.
"Then his voice deepened, his eyes shone, as we remember
him in his noblest moments, as he said: 'One hymn I think
supreme.' Emerson threw back his head, as he always did
when his attention was arrested, and waited. Doctor
Holmes repeated the first verse:

'Thou hidden Love of God, whose height,
    Whose depth unfathomed, no man knows!
I see from far thy beauteous light;
    Inly I sigh for thy repose;
My heart is pained, nor can it be
At rest, till it finds rest in thee.'

'I know—I know,' exclaimed Emerson. 'That is the supreme hymn!'" Other stanzas are:

Is there a thing beneath the sun,
    That strives with thee my heart to share?
Ah, tear it thence, and reign alone,
    The Lord of every motion there!
Then shall my heart from earth be free,
When it hath found repose in thee.

Each moment draw from earth away
    My heart, that lowly waits thy call;
Speak to my inmost soul, and say,
    "I am thy Love, thy God, thy All!"
To feel thy power, to hear thy voice,
To taste thy love, be all my choice.

This hymn was written by Tersteegen in 1729, and a few years later, while living in Savannah, John Wesley translated it into English.

We are interested in Count Zinzendorf because he wrote some very fine hymns, and, still more, because of his influence on John and Charles Wesley. As we shall presently see, these apostles of the evangelical revival learned from Zinzendorf and his fellow Moravians the power of sacred song, and they used it with the most blessed results in the great movement that was just beginning in England.

Nicolaus Ludwig Zinzendorf (1700-1760) belonged to the nobility of Saxony and was reared in affluence. But he inherited an intensely religious nature, and court life never appealed to him. As a mere school-boy he showed the bent of his mind by organizing among his companions the "Order of the Mustard Seed," which planned to do Christian service, especially in heathen lands. One day, in an art gallery, he saw a picture of Jesus wearing a crown of thorns, and the words, "All this I have done for thee; what hast thou done for me?" So deeply impressed was he that, as he expressed it, "From this time I had but one passion, and that was He, only He."

In those days the Moravians in their settlement at Herrnhut were a feeble and struggling people. But their forms of piety mightily attracted Zinzendorf, and he threw in his lot with them and became virtually the founder of the Moravian Church, as it has been known ever since. There, in the midst of his work, his foes brought about his banishment. For ten years he was an exile, but never idle. He carried his missionary activities far and wide, spending three years in the colony of Pennsylvania, where, in places like Bethlehem and Nazareth, his name is held in highest honor.

While of the more than two thousand hymns that Zinzendorf wrote very few are today in general use, those few are of rare merit. They breathe such a pure and trustful love for the Master that they appeal to Christians everywhere. "The first taught to the children in almost every German household," and a favorite in other lands, is the following:

Jesus, still lead on,
Till our rest be won;
And although the way be cheerless
We will follow, calm and fearless;
Guide us by thy hand
To our fatherland.

If the way be drear,
If the foe be near,
Let not faithless fears o'ertake us;
Let not faith and hope forsake us,
For, through many a foe,
To our home we go.

Jesus, still lead on,
Till our rest be won;
Heavenly Leader, still direct us,
Still support, console, protect us,
Till we safely stand
In our fatherland.

In 1739 Zinzendorf carried the gospel to the West Indies. As those island shores faded from sight on the voyage homeward, he wrote the lines:

Lord, I believe were sinners more
Than sands upon the ocean shore,
Thou hast for all a ransom paid,
For all a full atonement made.

This German hymn soon fell into the hands of John Wesley, whose English translation has been sung the world around for nearly two hundred years.

Still earlier, when Zinzendorf was only twenty-nine, appeared that hymn of mingled penitence and spiritual longing:

O thou to whose all-searching sight
The darkness shineth as the light,
Search, prove my heart; it pants for thee;
O burst these bonds and set it free.

Wash out its stains, refine its dross;
Nail my affections to the cross;
Hallow each thought; let all within
Be clean, as thou, my Lord, art clean.

> If rough and thorny be my way,
> My strength proportion to my day;
> Till toil and grief and pain shall cease
> Where all is calm and joy and peace.

Carl J. P. Spitta was perhaps the greatest German hymn writer of the nineteenth century; certainly he is the best known in American and English circles. In his student days rationalistic teachers tried to seduce him, but he broke away and returned to the simple faith of his boyhood. He entered the Lutheran ministry, where he became highly useful as a pastor, but most of all as a hymnist. Like so many poets, he began making verses when a mere child, and the gift steadily grew. His hymns, apart from their real literary merit, are so true to the gospel, so warm-hearted and sincere, that they struck a popular chord not only in Gemany, but far beyond. Of the many which have been rendered into English none is more often sung than the one on "Love to Christ":

> I know no life divided,
>   O Lord of life, from thee;
> In thee is life provided
>   For all mankind and me;
> I know no death, O Jesus,
>   Because I live in thee;
> Thy death it is that frees us
>   From death eternally.
>
> I fear no tribulation,
>   Since, whatso'er it be,
> It makes no separation
>   Between my Lord and me.
> If thou, my God and Teacher,
>   Vouchsafe to be my own,
> Though poor, I shall be richer
>   Than monarch on his throne.
>
> If, while on earth I wander,
>   My heart is light and blest,
> Oh, what shall I be yonder
>   In perfect peace and rest?
> O blessed thought in dying!
>   We go to meet the Lord,
> Where there shall be no sighing,
>   A kingdom our reward.

V

FRENCH HYMNS

ONLY A BRIEF reference need be made to the French hymns. In striking contrast to our enrichment from Germany, Protestant hymnody has received very little from French sources. The galaxy of brilliant hymnists of the Roman faith which distinguished England in the nineteenth century has had no counterpart in France; while hymns from Huguenot and other Protestant groups, as a rule, have been too limited both in number and religious scope to appeal to English translation. Two writers, however, call for special notice.

Madame Guyon, who died in 1717, was one of the most remarkable women that France ever produced. Though her entire life was spent in full communion with the Church of Rome, she was an ardent Quietist, and her peculiar views brought her into frequent and violent conflict with the ecclesiastical authorities. More than once she was under restraint, and at one time she was held a prisoner for four years in the Bastille. But her facile pen was never idle. Passionate consecration to God and spiritual fervor mingled with her deep mysticism and appear in all she wrote. Her sacred poems touched a responsive chord in the heart of William Cowper, and to him we are indebted for the English renderings. A pathetic significance clothes many of her hymns as we remember that they came to us from prison cell or from a bed of pain. The following lines are a special favorite:

> My Lord, how full of sweet content,
> I pass my years of banishment!
> Where'er I dwell, I dwell with thee
> In heaven, in earth, or on the sea.

To me remains nor place nor time;
My country is in every clime;
I can be calm and free from care
On any shore, since God is there.

While place we seek, or place we shun,
The soul finds happiness in none;
But with a God to guide our way
'Tis equal joy to go or stay.

Could I be cast where thou art not,
That were indeed a dreadful lot;
But regions none remote I call,
Secure of finding God in all.

César Malan was both the Watts and the Charles Wesley of French Protestantism. His sires were religious refugees from France to Geneva, and there he was born in 1787. He entered the ministry, but he was nearly thirty years old before he really came to himself. Then it was that he received a baptism of divine power which made of him a new man; and from that hour he was a torch in flame in the Master's service. His evangelistic tours carried him far and wide, on the Continent and in Britain; and wherever he went, in public and in private, he was a winner of souls. He early learned the untold value of sacred song, and he became the father of evangelical hymnody in France. Nearly one thousand hymns came from his pen, and he wrote melodies as well as words. Among his hymns which have passed into English, the one most widely known is the translation by Dr. George Bethune, opening with the lines,

It is not death to die,
To leave this weary road,
And midst the brotherhood on high
To be at home with God.

As we have already said, during the very time that under Lutheran influence hymns were in such high favor in one part of the Protestant fold, in other circles psalms were being sung with almost equal fervor. If France has given us few hymns, it is Frenchmen to whom we owe our first psalter in modern meter. The story of this psalter is of peculiar interest. Clement Marot lived in the first half of the sixteenth century. He was the court poet of France, and though his religious convictions were not the deepest, he sympathized with the Huguenot party. It was while writing his usual ballads that he conceived the notion of turning Hebrew psalms into French. The idea was novel, and presently, when copies in manuscript of thirty psalms were circulated in court circles, they sprang into instant favor. From the king down, the élite of the realm became psalmsingers, using the familiar ballad tunes. It is almost amusing to read of the eagerness with which individual psalms were seized. Prince Henry, a keen sportsman, demanded, especially for his own, "As the hart panteth after the waterbrooks;" while the king's mistress chose, "Out of the depths have I cried unto thee, O Lord." Whether or not in that gay and dissolute center any real good was done, we cannot say. We do know that Rome was angered at the Protestant leanings of Marot, and he had to flee for his life to Geneva.

It so happened that at this very time, John Calvin, himself a Frenchman and a religious refugee from his native land, was in Geneva, beginning his memorable work. He had the good sense to perceive that public worship without song would grow dull. At the same time his conscience and an austere taste would admit only Scripture passages. Thus hymn-singing, which the Lutherans were using with such notable effect, was ruled out: the psalms must suffice. He welcomed Marot, and at his request the poet increased the versified psalms to fifty, and they were published in 1543.

Marot died soon after, and at Calvin's solicitation, the scholarly Beza, another French refugee, turned the rest of the psalms into meter. At intervals tunes were added, and thus grew to completed form the Genevan Psalter, perhaps the most famous book of praise that the Christian Church ever produced. It gained immense popularity. Hundreds of editions appeared, and it was translated into various tongues. It became the psalm book of the Reformed Church on the Continent, and its influence on psalmody in England and Scotland and America remains to this day. Some of the original tunes are still used, chief among them, "Old Hundred," the most familiar and best-loved melody in the world.

In this matter of tunes Calvin again showed his severe taste. He sternly frowned upon the German chorale. It might be lively, but it was far too florid for the sanctuary. Nothing would do but the simple melody to be sung in unison. And yet song that would seem dull to modern ears was sweet and comforting four hundred years ago. An Englishman who had fled to Geneva to save his life declared (Lightwood, 24) that "a most interesting sight is offered in the city on week days, when the hour for service approaches. As soon as the first sound of the bell is heard all shops are closed, conversation ceases, business is put on one side, and from all parts people hasten to the nearest church. Arrived there, each one draws from his pocket a small book which contains some psalms with meter, and then the congregation sings before and after the sermon, while everyone testifies how great consolation is derived from this custom."

VI

ENGLISH METRICAL PSALMS AND PRE-WATTSIAN HYMNS

WE ARE NOW at the point where we pass over from the Continent of Europe to Britain, and turn to English song. If we trace the roots far enough, they lead us back to Anglo-Saxon days, when the gleesome, wandering minstrels sang knightly tales and sacred story; when, twelve centuries ago, Aldhem, devout and gifted bishop, stood at a bridgehead and sang his own songs, and then preached to the crowd of listeners. We think of John Wyclif and his followers. They were nicknamed "Lollards," perhaps from a word meaning "to sing softly" and sugggesting that they sang as well as preached in the tongue of the common people. But it is not till we come to the Reformation period, with its deep spiritual awakening, that we meet with religious song in its broader sense. The first echoes of the new movement to cross the Channel were from Lutheran Germany. We cannot help wondering, suppose there had been a Martin Luther in England, of his commanding leadership, and his love for hymns and music, what lines would Christian praise have followed? But England had no Luther, nor was she prepared for some of the drastic changes that the Germans promptly accepted. It was Calvin rather than Luther who set the model on British soil; the psalm instead of the hymn came into use both in England and Scotland, and afterward in America, and it continued in favor for two hundred years and more.

As psalm singing on the Continent started in court circles, it was much the same way in England. Sporadic attempts to versify the psalms had been made by Miles Coverdale in his "Goostly Psalmes and Spirituall Songes," and by others; but the definite beginning must be credited to Thomas Stern-

hold. He was Groom of the Robes to Henry VIII and also
to Edward VI. A man of refined taste as well as genuine
piety, he was disgusted with the lewd songs that he heard
all about him. Partly for his own solace and to encourage
something better, he used to versify psalms and play and
sing them at his organ; while sometimes the boy king would
listen with wonder and delight. Sternhold died in 1549, but
the work was gradually carried on by others, chiefly by John
Hopkins, of whom we know almost nothing except that he
was probably a clergyman and schoolmaster.

There was then completed and printed in 1562 what is
called the Old Version of the psalter. Two years later a similar psalm book appeared for the Scottish Church. While Edward was king, public psalm singing in England became
popular, only to be suppressed under "Bloody Mary." But
John Knox and his fellow Protestants, who fled to Geneva,
the home of psalmody, retained and improved the fine custom. Some of the best parts of the Old Version were written
by English refugees, and when Elizabeth was crowned it
was largely Genevan example and influence that restored the
psalms to England. They not only were quickly introduced
into many churches, but an eyewitness tells us, "You may
now see at St. Paul's Cross (adjoining the cathedral) after
service, six thousand persons, old and young, of both sexes,
all singing together and praising God."

The coming of the Sternhold and Hopkins, or Old Version, with its royal sanction, gave a further impetus to psalm
singing. The success of this book was astonishing. To be
sure, its literary style is beneath criticism. Samuel Wesley,
father of John, referred to many of the metrical renderings
as "scandalous doggerel," and other critics caustically spoke
of "Hopkins his jigges." While it gives us the noble "Old
Hundred," "All people that on earth do dwell," more often
we have hymns like these:

> They shall heap sorrow on their heads,
>   Which run as they were mad,
> To offer to the idoll-gods.
>   Alas, it is too bad.

or

> Why doost withdrawe thy hand aback,
>   And hide it in thy lappe?
> O plucke it out, and be not slack
>   To give thy foes a rappe!

But in spite of hopeless defects, it remained the accepted book of praise in England for one hundred and thirty-four years. And long after a better version appeared the old one still continued in wide and loving favor. The Sternhold and Hopkins book never found much acceptance in America. The Puritan emigrants brought it with them to New England, but they had never been satisfied with it. They wanted renderings in closer adherence to the Hebrew original, and so they made it their first business to prepare a version of their own, the famous "Bay Psalm Book." This held supreme place till the psalms and hymns of Watts came into use.

In 1696, two Irishmen, Nahum Tate and Nicholas Brady, both of the Established Church, brought out what is known as the New Version of metrical psalms. Tate was Poet Laureate, though his talents were moderate, while Brady was a clergyman of ordinary standing. This version carried the royal permission to be used in churches, but it made slow progress, and in many rural parishes, the Old Version, with its hallowed associations, never gave place to the New. Although, taken as a whole, the New Version could not boast of any pronounced poetic excellence, yet it was a real advance over the other. It had a literary flavor which commended it to people of refined taste, and especially in the Church of England it steadily grew in popular regard. In 1789, it was officially adopted by the Protestant Episcopal Church in America, and was bound up with the Prayer Book.

Though today almost unknown, we do well to remember that some of its choicest renderings of the psalms, such as the 34th, "Thro' all the changing scenes of life," and the 42nd, "As pants the hart for cooling streams," enrich our modern hymnals. In 1702, a supplement of six hymns, no doubt by Tate, was added to the psalter. The first of the six is that lovely Christmas carol, sung the world over,

> While shepherds watched their flocks by night
> All seated on the ground.

These few hymns have the honor to be the first received into recognized use in the Church of England.

Confirmed, as Britain was in the use of psalms, the people had too much of the lyrical spirit to continue indefinitely in the old way; they must have something more singable. Moreover, the feeling grew that the psalms, with all their merit, represented only the Old Testament; they carried no Christian message. A change for the better was bound to come. For many years now, English hymnody has outdistanced anything the world has ever known.

We usually think of Isaac Watts as leader of the long line of English hymn writers; but we must not ignore the rare souls that came before and who helped to prepare the way for Watts. For many years religious songs on a variety of subjects, and intended for use in the home, had made their appearance from time to time. The art of music was cultivated to a considerable extent in Elizabeth's reign, and while singing in unison was the rule at church, in the family circle it was not at all uncommon to sing all four parts. In 1583 there appeared a small book by William Hunnis, a court official. It contained the Penitential Psalms in meter, and, along with other religious pieces, what he called a "Handful of Honisuckles." Among the "Honisuckles" is this quaint little song:

> O Jesu sweet, a little thing
>   Sometimes doth vex me sore,
> And makes me slow to give thee thanks;
>   Ah, woe is me therefore.
>
> Jesu, again sometimes I think
>   Full stronglie for to stand,
> But when a little trouble comes,
>   I straight fall under hand.
>
> Thus, Jesu, see a small thing makes
>   Temptation great to be,
> My weakness, Jesu, doo behold,
>   And mercie have on me. Amen.

Hunnis also set tunes to his "Honisuckles," and we have here the earliest modern use of the "Amen" at the end of hymns.

At a later date came George Wither, soldier as well as poet, who died at a good old age in 1667. He was a voluminous writer, giving to the world more than a hundred books and pamphlets. Whether in peace or in war his muse took no rest, but his hymns, many of them of real beauty, were suited to family or to private devotion rather than to the church. In his "Halleluyah" are two hundred and thirty-three hymns on as many different subjects, touching almost every conceivable experience from the cradle to the grave. For example he wrote "A Rocking Hymn":

> Sweet baby, sleep: what ails my dear?
>   What ails my darling thus to cry?
> Be still, my child, and lend thine ear,
>   To hear me sing thy lullaby.
> My pretty lamb, forbear to weep;
> Be still, my dear; sweet baby, sleep.

> When God with us was dwelling here,
>   In little babes he took delight;
> Such innocents as thou, my dear!
>   Are ever precious in his sight.
> Sweet baby, then forbear to weep;
> Be still, my babe; sweet baby, sleep.

More to our present purpose is the work of George Herbert (1593-1632). We think of him as a devoted country parson, during his short life, day by day cheerfully going about his humble duties. He wrote a book of sacred verse, called "The Temple," which so appealed to the Wesleys that they introduced many of its poems into one of their hymn books, where they were long treasured by the Methodists. Selections from Herbert appear in most of our modern collections. Their real loveliness, coupled with a quaint simplicity, gives them a peculiar charm. A prime favorite is the poem entitled, "The Elixir, or Philosopher's Stone," based on the old-time idea of the magic secret for transmuting the base into the precious.   The opening lines are just as Herbert wrote them:

> Teach me, my God and King,
>   In all things thee to see,
> And what I do in anything
>   To do it as for thee.

The other stanzas, as sung today, have been largely recast.
In their original form they run as follows:

> All may of this partake,
>   Nothing can be so mean
> Which with this tincture, "for thy sake,"
>   Will not grow bright and clean.

> A servant with this clause
>   Makes drudgery divine;
> Who sweeps a room as for thy laws,
>   Makes that the action fine.

> This is the famous stone
>   That turneth all to gold,
> For that which God doth touch and own
>   Cannot for less be told.

Another gem from this same poet, occasionally sung, is the following:

> Let all the world in every corner sing
>   My God and King!
> The heavens are not too high,
> His praise may thither fly;
> The earth is not too low,
> His praises there may grow.
> Let all the world in every corner sing
>   My God and King!

> Let all the world in every corner sing
>   My God and King!
> The Church with psalms must shout,
> No door can keep them out;
> But above all my heart
> Must bear the longest part.
> Let all the world in every corner sing
>   My God and King!

> Let all the world in every corner sing
>   My God and King!
> The Father with the Son
> And Spirit, three in One,
> One everlasting Lord,
> Be evermore adored!
> Let all the world in every corner sing
>   My God and King!

At the time of his death in 1683, Samuel Crossman, was Dean of Bristol Cathedral. He wrote especially for young men, and it is in this connection that we find his hymns. They are in a minor key, and while breathing a sweet assurance, they strike us as more adapted to advanced age than to youth. They are better known in England than in America. From a poem on "Heaven" we take these stanzas:

> Sweet place; sweet place alone!
>   The court of God most High,
> The heaven of heavens, the throne
>   Of spotless majesty!
> O happy place! when shall I be,
> My God, with thee, to see thy face?
>
> The stranger homeward bends,
>   And sigheth for his rest;
> Heaven is my home, my friends
>   Lodge there in Abraham's breast.
> O happy place! when shall I be,
> My God, with thee, to see thy face?

It has been said that "rarely did Watts rise to the height of thought and beauty found in Mason's hymns." (W. Garrett Horder in "The Hymn Lover," page 87.) This is high praise and perhaps not unmerited. Certain it is that John Mason's verses were so superior that they were among the earliest to win favor in the Church of England. And, still more, they made a strong impress on other writers. Watts was twenty years old when Mason died in 1694 and was on the threshold of his brilliant career. His own work was influenced by that of the older poet, and this was likewise true of Charles Wesley at a later time. Among the best known of Mason's hymns is that lovely vesper song, beginning,

> Now from the altar of my heart
>   Let incense flames arise;
> Assist me, Lord, to offer up
>   Mine evening sacrifice;

and the lines,

> My Lord, my Love, was crucified,
>   He all the pain did bear;
> But in the sweetness of his rest
>   He makes his servant share.

A favored place is held by the hymn closing with the stanza,

> To whom, Lord, should I sing, but thee,
>   The Maker of my tongue!
> Lo, other lords would seize on me,
>   But I to thee belong.
> As waters haste into their sea,
>   And earth unto its earth,
> So let my soul return to thee
>   From whom it had its birth.

We must bear in mind that the great bulk of the hymns written in England prior to the eighteenth century were never sung and were never designed for such use. Whatever the after years may have done with them, in the intent of the author they were sacred poetry for devotional reading. In the case of Richard Baxter (1615-1691), however, it seems to have been otherwise. We think of him as the writer of "The Saints' Everlasting Rest," that great devotional classic, and the faithful minister of Christ who made it his life purpose

> To preach as though he'd never preach again,
> And as a dying man to dying men.

He was also a lover of sacred song. He became "the leader at once of the Presbyterians and of the movement to introduce hymn singing into the churches." (L. F. Benson in "The English Hymn," page 84.) He set an example by writing hymns of his own, apparently intended for public use. The best-loved among them is from the longer poem, "The Covenant and Confidence of Faith":

> Lord, it belongs not to my care
>   Whether I die or live;
> To love and serve thee is my share,
>   And this thy grace must give.
>
> If life be long, I will be glad
>   That I may long obey;
> If short, yet why should I be sad
>   To soar to endless day?
>
> Christ leads me through no darker rooms
>   Than he went through before;
> He that into God's kingdom comes
>   Must enter by this door.
>
> My knowledge of that life is small;
>   The eye of faith is dim;
> But 'tis enough that Christ knows all,
>   And I shall be with him.

When this saintly man lay on his deathbed waiting for release from pain, he murmured, "It is not for me to prescribe; when thou wilt; what thou wilt; how thou wilt." Thus he lived and died.

In the story of English hymn writers Thomas Ken holds a unique place, not for the quantity of his verse, but for the amazing use that has been made of it. Quite apart from his literary work, he was a notable character. Born in 1637, and early left an orphan, he found a warm welcome in the home of his gifted brother-in-law, Izaak Walton, of angling fame. When a lad of fourteen he entered Winchester College; that famous school was then nearly three hundred years old. Later, he became a priest in the Anglican Church, and, advancing from one post of honor to another, he was finally appointed by Charles II Bishop of Bath and Wells. In many cases such promotion would have meant little, but not so with Ken. One of his outstanding qualities was a moral courage that knew no fear or favor. Small in body, he had the spirit of the ancient prophets, and time and again he rebuked sin in the seats of the mighty. Charles II knew this, but he admired "little Ken," as he called him, and made him a court chaplain, and enjoyed his sermons, saying, "I must go and hear little Ken tell me of my faults."

On one occasion, while Ken was prebendary at Winchester, the king, with his mistress, visited the place, and it was planned that Nell Gwynne should lodge at the prelate's home. When Ken heard of it he indignantly refused to allow such a woman as a guest under his roof. "Not for his kingdom" would he comply with the royal demands. But Charles must have respected his chaplain, for later, when a vacancy occurred, he made him a bishop. Ken was one of the seven bishops committed to the Tower because he would not bow to the tyranny of James II, and still later he was among those who refused to take the oath of allegiance to William III, though this act cost him his episcopal seat. Firm as a rock in his loyalty to conscience, he was likewise the soul of gentle, loving saintliness. He merited the title, "Seraphic Prelate."

When a young man of twenty-eight, after an absence of several years he returned to Winchester, where he soon became a Fellow of the College. Naturally he felt a big brother's interest in the boys of the school, where he himself had spent such happy days. He knew their needs, their hopes and temptations, and in 1674 he prepared for them a "Manual of Prayer." In this small book, along with other advice, he urged the boys each day to "be sure to sing the Morning and Evening Hymns in your chamber devoutly." Probably it refers to his own hymns, afterward so famous.

He was a lover of music and it was his habit to rise in the morning at two or three o'clock, for prayer and meditation, and to begin the day with singing a hymn, accompanying himself on an organ in his college room. His hymns did not appear in the "Manual of Prayer" at first, but were most likely given to the boys in leaflet form. They were not printed in the "Manual" till 1694. These three hymns, for

Morning, Evening and Midnight, originally consisted of
thirty-seven stanzas in all, and each hymn closed with the
familiar doxology, "Praise God from whom all blessings
flow." They were slow in coming into use, chiefly because
the age of hymn singing had hardly begun; and it was not
until the nineteenth century that they found general acceptance.

Today there are few Protestant hymn books in the English-speaking world that do not contain selected verses from
the "Morning and Evening Hymns." Ken himself was
especially fond of his morning song; general favor leans to
the evening.

In the very nature of the case, the "Midnight Hymn" is
rarely used, nor is it quite equal to the others. In part it
runs as follows:

> My God, now I from sleep awake,
> The sole possession of me take;
> Let no vain fancy me illude,
> No one impure desire intrude.
>
> O may I always ready stand
> With my lamp burning in my hand;
> May I in sight of heaven rejoice,
> Whene'er I hear the Bridegroom's voice!
>
> All praise to thee in light arrayed,
> Who light thy dwelling place hast made,
> A boundless Ocean of bright beams,
> From thy all-glorious Godhead streams.
>
> Shine on me, Lord, new life impart,
> Fresh ardors kindle in my heart;
> One ray of thy all-quickening light
> Dispels the sloth and clouds of night.

The doxology holds a place supreme, as the most widely
sung verse of sacred praise. Ken wrote a number of hymns,
but only the three we have mentioned have lived. And they
are enough, for in their charming simplicity and universal
appeal they must ever remain the earliest really great hymns
in our English tongue. As the end drew near, Ken faced

death with a cheerful heart. For years, wherever he went, he had carried his shroud with him, that he might always be ready when the last messenger came. Twelve poor men bore his body to its resting place, and his wish was carried out, to be buried "in the churchyard . . . under the East Window of the chancel, just at sun-rising."

VII

ISAAC WATTS AND HIS CONTEMPORARIES

S THE SEVENTEENTH CENTURY wore on, there developed, especially in Nonconformist circles, a growing restlesness in the matter of psalm singing. What at first had been practiced with real enthusiasm had become dull and lifeless. It was bad enough in the city, but worse in the country. A dismal picture is drawn of the "whining, tooting, yelling or screeching" in the ordinary rural church (Lightwood, 76). So few congregations had sufficient psalm books, and so many of the people were too ignorant to use them even had they been provided, that the psalms were "lined out." At best it was a weariness of soul, and moreover it led to absurdities, as when, for example, a pastor or clerk read the line, and the congregation solemnly sang it, "The Lord will come and he will not," followed by the line, "Keep silence but speak out." The tunes in common use were few and the same tune might be sung in the same church twenty times in a single week. Or, still worse, worshipers might insist on doing their own selecting, and then various tunes would be running at the same time. Everywhere people of superior taste were groaning for something better, and yet they were loath to break with the past. Increasing numbers of sacred poems had been appearing, which, though intended primarily for private devotions, yet were really suited to public song.

The time was ripening for a change. What was needed was strong leadership. The opening of the eighteenth century was a dreary time for religion. With the passing of Baxter, Owen and other heroes, Puritanism lost its glory. A type of unitarian belief threw its withering spell over many churches. Dissenters and churchmen alike were in the clutches of a chill formalism. Evangelical sermons were

93

rarely heard, and no wonder, when men like Robert South, the greatest preacher of his day, never ceased to warn their hearers against "enthusiasm" as "worse than popery," —"a mother from whose teeming womb have issued some of the vilest, foulest . . . practices and opinions that the nature of man was ever poisoned and polluted with" (Pamph. 4-3).

Even orthodoxy was too dead to grip men. Amid such conditions came the slow dawning of a new era of sacred song, which, in turn, was the harbinger of the rich spiritual life which would one day overspread England. Among the pioneers was Benjamin Keach. He was pastor of a Baptist church in London. With others, the Baptists had been bitterly averse to hymn singing in public worship, but Keach felt differently. It was a long struggle. He began with a hymn at the communion service; after six years he ventured to use one on thanksgiving days. After fourteen years more of perseverance and debate, he was allowed to add a hymn at the regular public worship. It was brought at the close of the service, so that the disgruntled ones might withdraw before the evil thing came on. But even so, an angry minority left altogether and started a songless church. There were similar experiences elsewhere. In the meantime hymn collections had been making a timid appearance, one by Keach himself, the "Spiritual Melody," containing no less than three hundred hymns, showing what a supply of material was already at hand. And now, following divers John the Baptists, came the great leader who was to do for sacred song in England something akin to what Luther had done in Germany two hundred years before.

Had we chanced to visit the little town of Southampton in the fall of 1674, we might have seen a young woman sitting on the stone steps of the village jail, holding a puny babe, her first born, in her arms. It was Mrs. Watts with the tiny Isaac. She was waiting to be admitted to the jail to see her husband. His only crime was that he was a Dissenter and active in the exercise of his faith. Those were harsh days, and dissent from the Established Church sometimes involved cruel cost. The son never forgot the treatment his father received, and a few years later when wealthy friends offered to pay his expenses at Oxford or Cambridge to prepare for the Anglican ministry, he politely but firmly refused.

Baby Isaac was born on July 17, 1674, only a few weeks before Milton died. Ideas on education, in those days were different from our own; and when he was four years old the boy was set to work on Latin and a little later on Greek and Hebrew. At the age of fifteen he entered the Academy at Stoke Newington, a suburb of London, where he was a hard student for five years. Then he returned to his Southampton home for a couple of years and, as we shall presently see, they proved to be two of the most significant years of his life. After further study he entered the ministry and when only twenty-eight he became pastor in Mark Lane, the leading Independent Church in London. But it soon appeared that his health was unequal to the task and an associate was chosen to assist him. Till his death at the age of seventy-four Watts remained the nominal pastor-in-chief, preaching whenever possible. But he was a frail little body, not much above five feet high, a lifelong invalid, and much of the time an acute sufferer.

So far as outward circumstance was concerned, the greatest blessing that ever came to him was when he entered the home of Sir Thomas Abney. Sir Thomas had a magnificent estate a few miles out of London. He knew and admired Watts and he invited him to spend a week at his home. The stay was so delightful that the guest was urged to remain longer, and then the visit of a few days was lengthened to thirty-six years, till the close of Watts's life. The plan was ideal. Watts never married, and, because of his physical weakness, life would have become increasingly hard and lonely if he had lived by himself. But in this palatial home with all its comforts, where he had perfect freedom and loving friends to meet his every want with almost reverent devotion, he was care-free, and the passing years brought him rare joy.

Nor were the benefits all on one side. On a certain occasion when Lady Huntingdon called on Doctor Watts, he said to her, "Madame, you have come to see me on a very remarkable day. This day, thirty years ago, I came hither to the house of my good friend, Sir Thomas, intending to spend but a week under his hospitable roof, and I have extended my visit to thirty long years." "Sir," said his gracious hostess, Lady Abney, "what you term a long thirty years' visit, I consider as the shortest visit my family ever received." (Gregory, p. 124.) What light it throws on the charming personality of Isaac Watts! The earthly close of this beautiful life came a few days before Christmas in 1748. Very appropriately, the burial took place in old Bunhill Fields, London, perhaps the most hallowed cemetery in the world, where lies the dust of Bunyan, Defoe, Susannah Wesley, and scores of others, renowned chiefly in the work of the Kingdom.

Watts might have lived a devout, amiable and useful life, but his name would long since have been forgotten, had it not been that he also rendered a service so notable that it lifted him to a seat among the immortals. He was born with a soul for harmony, and from childhood his thoughts took to rhyme. Every Sunday he faithfully attended service at the meeting-house, but the dull, lifeless droning of the psalms, or the singing of William Barton's hymns, which latterly came into use, made no appeal.

Presently his opportunity came. He was twenty years old; his academy days were over and he was back home once more with his Southampton friends. One Sunday he was complaining of the hymns. "Very well," said his father, "then give us something better." The young man eagerly accepted the challenge, and quickly wrote his first production. It was used at the next service and the people were so delighted that they besought him for a new one every Sunday. He complied, and thus a large number were composed. All of them were in manuscript and "lined out" for singing. His initial venture has a peculiar interest. He entitled it, "A

New Song to the Lamb That Was Slain," and while it was by no means equal to many that he afterward wrote, it was superior to most which were then in circulation:

> Behold the glories of the Lamb
>   Amidst his Father's throne;
> Prepare new honors for his name,
>   And songs before unknown.

> Now to the Lamb, that once was slain,
>   Be endless blessings paid;
> Salvation, glory, joy, remain
>   Forever on thy head.

> Thou hast redeemed our souls with blood,
>   Hast set the prisoner free,
> Hast made us kings and priests to God,
>   And we shall reign with thee.

It was during these two memorable years when he was entering the twenties that Watts wrote the great bulk of his hymns. They were laid aside and might have been forgotten, had it not been for the younger brother Enoch, who urged their publication. They were given to the world in 1707 in the little book, "Hymns and Spiritual Songs." Watts received fifty dollars for the copyright, a pitiful sum when contrasted with the fortunes publishers made in after years. It was this book that created an epoch in Christian praise.

Watts is often spoken of as the "Father of the English hymn," but this is an error. England had hymns before Watts was born, and even had he never appeared, no doubt, in time, it would have become what it is today, a land of hymn singers. But it was Watts who gave the compelling impetus to a movement already emerging. While others had made timid gestures, he strode forward with a daring, an assurance, born of perfect confidence. He believed in himself, in the people, and in the new form of praise. His "Hymns and Spiritual Songs" gave the hymn a definite standing. It was the first *people's hymn book* in England, and for that country it forever settled the future of sacred song.

And yet the churches kept Watts "on probation" for some years, because of their scruples against using in public worship hymns of "human composure." What helped the hymns was the appearance in 1719 of "The Psalms of David Imitated in the Language of the New Testament," also by Watts, and in some ways the crowning work of his life. Happily he attempted no translation where so many had tried and failed; but he brought David down to the eighteenth century and caused him to speak as a Christian Englishman, while with skillful touch he transformed Judah and Israel into England and Scotland, and the Land of Canaan into Great Britain. Thus his "Imitation," while retaining much of the spirit and sacredness of the ancient psalms, became adapted to present-day needs. Many of our best-loved hymns are found among the "Psalms Imitated;" and more, the Imitations made such an appeal that they greatly aided in the passing from the old-time metrical psalms, so dear to the people, to the new-time hymns.

Watts might be held at arm's length, but only for a while. Let some shake the head dubiously and others openly scoff at what they dubbed "Watts Whims;" let the poet Young with biting sarcasm speak of "Isaac, a brother of the canting strain" (Pamph. C;51); still Watts grew in public favor, and when once he was accepted it was with a fervor unparalleled in Christian hymnody. There was a mighty appeal in his verse. Doddridge wrote to him of the effect on a congregation of his own. They had been singing, "Give me the wings of faith to rise within the veil": "I had the satisfaction to observe tears in the eyes of several of the people; and after the service was over, some of them told me they were not able to sing, so deeply were their minds affected! They were most of them poor people, who work for their living, yet, on the mention of your name, I found . . . that your psalms and hymns were almost their daily entertainment." Thus it continued.

Especially among the dissenters on both sides of the ocean Watts swept all before him. In his hold on the reverential devotion of the people, even the Bible took small precedence. If a hymn by another writer was announced, there were sure to be some who would sit down and refuse to sing. This supremacy continued for more than one hundred years, and if it has now lapsed it is because the standard of hymn writing has so risen and the wealth of hymns so increased that the churches are keener in selecting only the best for their collections. But it was Watts who led the way.

Even the most ardent admirer must admit that of the hundreds of hymns from the pen of Isaac Watts, very many are inferior in literary quality. When he soared he attained superlative heights; but, unhappily, he did not always soar. Much that he wrote was commonplace, as when he described God fashioning the human body:

> He spoke, and straight our hearts and brains
>   In all their motions rose;
> "Let blood," said he, "flow round the veins,"
>   And round the veins it flows.

All through Watts's hymns we find faulty rhyme; he is charged with "feebleness" and "prosaic and slovenly writing;" and we cannot deny it. But be it remembered he was a pioneer with very little to guide him. He was the soul of modesty, always insisting he was not a poet; and further, so intent was he on bringing his verses within the comprehension of the humblest Christian, that he deliberately lowered their literary excellence. As he said, "Some of the beauties of poesy are neglected and some wilfully defaced." The wonder is not that some of his work is poor, but that the average is so high.

At one time enemies started the rumor that Watts had a dangerous leaning toward the Unitarian faith. How absurd, in view of the fact that no less than one hundred and seven of his hymns dwell on the glory of the divine Christ. He was trained in rigid Calvinism and we might expect many references to this type of theology, but rarely do we find a word which could offend even the most sensitive soul. His heart was too tender to sing of infant damnation, nor did he exclude anyone from saving grace:

> While the lamp holds out to burn
> The vilest sinner may return.

He was tolerant for his time, saying, "I am persuaded there is a breadth in the narrow road to heaven, and persons may tread more than seven abreast on it" (Pamph. D-5).

Watts was not an evangelist as we often use the term. He never felt the mighty urge which led Wesley to view the world as his parish. And yet no one could have longed more than he to see men saved, as when he sang,

> Who can describe the joys that rise
> Through all the courts of Paradise,
> To see a prodigal return,
> To see an heir of glory born?

And at a time, long before the spiritual welfare of the heathen had become a burden on the heart of the Church, he wrote the hymn which has been used oftener than any other on missionary occasions:

> Jesus shall reign where'er the sun
> Does his successive journeys run.

No writer ever lived whose hymns were so saturated with the Scriptures as Watts. Quite apart from his psalm imitation, scores of his hymns are simply brief sermons in verse and there is scarcely one not founded on a text.

Complaint has often been made of his large use of the minor key. True, he has much to say of "the weeping eye" and the "straight and thorny road," and we hear his wail:

> Our days, alas! our mortals days,
> Are short and wretched too;
> "Evil and few," the patriarch says,
> And well the patriarch knew.

But many even of his somber hymns close with the note of faith and courage, as in the lines,

> Swift as an eagle cuts the air,
>   We'll mount aloft to thine abode;
> On wings of love our souls shall fly,
>   Nor tire amidst the heavenly road.

And for two hundred years the people of God have been singing,

> Come let us join our cheerful songs
>   With angels round the throne;
> Ten thousand thousand are their tongues
>   But all their joys are one.

Can we ask for lovelier lines than these?

> My God, the spring of all my joys,
>   The life of my delights,
> The glory of my brightest days,
>   And comfort of my nights.
>
> In darkest shades, if he appear
>   My dawning is begun;
> He is my soul's sweet morning-star
>   And he my rising sun.

The same pen that pictured with gruesome realism a dying person,

> His quivering lip hangs feebly down,
>   His pulses faint and few;
> Then speechless, with a doleful groan,
>   He bids the world adieu,

also wrote,

> Jesus can make a dying bed
>   Feel soft as downy pillows are,
> While on his breast I lean my head,
>   And breathe my life out sweetly there.

The author of those lugubrious words that had such a strange fascination for our fathers,

> Hark from the tombs a doleful sound,
>   My ears, attend the cry;
> Ye living men, come view the ground
>   Where you must shortly lie,

also gave us that hymn of sweet and abiding comfort,

> There is a land of pure delight,
>   Where saints immortal reign;
> Infinite day excludes the night,
>   And pleasures banish pain.
>
> There everlasting spring abides
>   And never-withering flowers;
> Death, like a narrow sea, divides
>   This heavenly land from ours.
>
> Sweet fields beyond the swelling flood
>   Stand dressed in living green;
> So to the Jews old Canaan stood,
>   While Jordan rolled between.
>
> Could we but climb where Moses stood,
>   And view the landscape o'er,
> Not Jordan's stream, nor death's cold flood,
>   Should fright us from the shore.

Tradition says that the language of this hymn was suggested to Watts by the view across the "narrow sea" not far from Southampton to the neighboring Isle of Wight. The "swelling flood" driven by wind and tide, the "sweet fields . . . in living green" and the climate of "everlasting spring" were doubtless parts of a picture at which he had often looked. We need not be unduly distressed when he tells us:

> My thoughts on awful subjects roll,
>   Damnation and the dead,

or with his lurid description of the "dismal hell" with its

> Eternal plagues and heavy chains,
>   Tormenting racks, and fiery coals,
> And darts to inflict immortal pain,
>   Dyed in the blood of damnèd souls.

For long decades effusions of a so-called "alarming" character continued to appear from many pens and were heartily sung in the churches.

Undoubtedly Watts is at his best when dealing with the majestic. The might of God appealed to him, as did the love of God to Charles Wesley. It is Watts who sings of the

> Eternal Power, whose high abode
> Becomes the grandeur of a God,

and the Monarch whose "sounding chariot shakes the sky" and "who treads the worlds beneath his feet." We freely grant that Watts's hymns have their serious limitations, but Christian praise could ill afford to lose those close rivals to Ken's Morning and Evening Hymns:

> Lord, in the morning thou shalt hear
> My voice ascending high.

> Thus far the Lord hath led me on,
> Thus far his power prolongs my days;
> And every evening shall make known
> Some fresh memorial of his grace,

or Sabbath hymns as,

> Sweet is the work, my God, my King,
> To praise thy name, give thanks and sing.

> To spend a day with thee on earth
> Exceeds a thousand days of mirth.

Think of the Advent song, like the peal of Christmas bells,

> Joy to the world, the Lord is come!

and the militant hymn,

> Am I a soldier of the cross,
> A follower of the Lamb?

Nor will the Church ever outgrow

> When I can read my title clear
> To mansions in the skies.

And what shall we say of that noble ascription, regarded by many as Watts's greatest hymn, based on the Ninetieth Psalm and clothed in all the solemn grandeur of its great original?

> O God, our help in ages past,
> Our hope for years to come,
> Our shelter from the stormy blast,
> And our eternal home!

And that other hymn, also supreme, which has an abiding place in the communion service of the Church:

> When I survey the wondrous cross
>   On which the Prince of glory died,
> My richest gain I count but loss,
>   And pour contempt on all my pride.

The last hymn that John Wesley announced, when he preached at City Road Chapel only a week before his death, was one by Watts which he had loved all through life:

> I'll praise my Maker while I've breath,
> And when my voice is lost in death,
>   Praise shall employ my nobler powers;
> My days of praise shall ne'er be past,
> While life, and thought, and being last,
>   Or immortality endures.

Wesley sang it again a few hours before the end, and once more, as the angel of death stooped low, the aged man murmured, "I'll praise—I'll praise."

We must not leave Watts without mentioning his "Divine and Moral Songs for Children." They were written during his long stay in the Abney family, whose junior members as well as the parents, were very dear to him. The "Songs" soon became immensely popular, and for more than a century were found in every home. The "Cradle Hymn" is one of the sweetest lullabies ever written:

> Hark! my dear, lie still and slumber,
>   Holy angels guard thy bed!
> Heavenly blessings, without number,
>   Gently falling on thy head.
>
> *   *   *   *
>
> I could give thee thousand kisses,
>   Hoping what I most desire;
> Not a mother's fondest wishes
>   Can to greater joys aspire!

On a summer day, June 26, 1702, in an airless chamber of

an old London house, was born a baby boy. They thought he was dead, and the tiny body was laid to one side for burial. But a neighbor noticed a slight movement; the child was tenderly nursed, and thus there was saved to the world Philip Doddridge. Nineteen children had preceded him in that family circle, but all save one, a sickly little girl, died when quite young. No wonder that Philip was reared with lavish devotion. His parents were devout people, and the mother, herself the daughter of a clergyman, gave close care to the boy's religious training. The chimney corner was lined with blue Dutch tiles showing Bible scenes, and, with these pictures as texts, the mother spent many an hour in telling Philip the wonderful stories of old.

But soon both father and mother were taken away, and the young orphan was thrown out upon the world. Happily kind friends came to his relief, and with their aid he obtained an education which prepared him for the ministry. He began preaching when he was only twenty, in an obscure parish with a few farmers as an audience. "I have not so much as a tea table in my diocese—and but one hoop petticoat in the whole circuit; and were it not for talking to the cattle, admiring the poultry, and preaching twice every Sabbath, I should certainly lose the organ of speech." Presently we find him settled in Northampton as pastor of an Independent church, and here he remained to the close of his ministry.

He was an unwearied toiler. In addition to his regular parish duties, he conducted a seminary where hundreds of young men were trained, most of them for Dissenting pulpits. He wrote much. To this day his "Family Expositor" is occasionally found as a prized heirloom in old family libraries. Still more important was the "Rise and Progress of Religion in the Soul." It is scarcely too much to say that this was the most valuable devotional book of the eighteenth century, and its influence in that age of spiritual dearth was enormous.

But Doddridge is chiefly remembered for his hymns. He

was the junior of Watts by many years, and Watts's hymns
were just coming into use, as Doddridge began his ministry.
The two men grew to be fast friends, and the younger became the ardent admirer and disciple of the older. The
hymns of Doddridge are fewer in number, nor do they ever
equal Watts at his best; but their literary excellence and
rich devotional spirit have secured for some of them a permanent place among the songs of the Church. Most of
them were written for use at the close of service, and were
intended to present in this striking form the essence of the
sermon. For example, after a message on "Casting all your
care upon him," an added impression was made by singing,

> How gentle God's commands!
> How kind his precepts are!
> Come, cast your burdens on the Lord,
> And trust his constant care.

Following a sermon on "The Eternal Sabbath," it was quite
appropriate to sing,

> Lord of the Sabbath, hear our vows,
> On this thy day, in this thy house,
> And own, as grateful sacrifice,
> The songs which from thy servants rise.

One Sunday Doddridge preached on "Suffer the little
children to come unto me," and then read his own hymn, a
favorite with us on baptismal occasions, opening with the
verse,

> See Israel's gentle Shepherd stand
> With all-engaging charms;
> Hark, how he calls the tender lambs
> And folds them in his arms!

A sermon entitled, "Pressing on in the Christian Race," was
enforced by the lines "ringing like a trumpeter's note to start
the athletes":

> Awake, my soul, stretch every nerve,
> And press with vigor on.

What many regard as the best of the Doddridge hymns is

the one written for Christmas, 1735, which ranks among the noblest of our Nativity songs:

> Hark the glad sound! the Saviour comes,
>   The Saviour promised long!
> Let every heart prepare a throne,
>   And every voice a song.

That outburst of spiritual rapture, "O happy day, that fixed my choice," has been the birthday pæan of unnumbered souls. As written by Doddridge, it had no refrain; none was needed. Whether heard in mission hall or in stately cathedral, it carried the same blessed witness. Queen Victoria was so fond of it that at her request it was sung at the confirmation of one of her children.

What has given to the hymns of Doddridge much of their appeal may be traced to the rich experience from which they sprang. He was a man of singular purity of character and of unfailing communion with God. It was a personal testimony when he wrote:

> Return my soul, and take thy rest
> Upon thy Heavenly Father's breast;
> Indulge me, Lord, in that repose,
> The soul which loves thee only knows.
>
> Lodged in thine arms I fear no more
> The tempest's howl, the billows' roar;
> Those storms must shake the Almighty's seat,
> Which violate the saints' retreat.

Doddridge was especially happy in his New Year's hymns. The following is one of the noblest from any pen, and fully merits the wide use that is made of it:

> Great God, we sing that mighty hand
> By which supported still we stand;
> The opening year thy mercy shows;
> That mercy crowns it till its close.
>
> By day, by night, at home, abroad,
> Still are we guarded by our God;
> By his incessant bounty fed,
> By his unerring counsel led.

> With grateful hearts the past we own;
> The future all to us unknown,
> We to thy guardian care commit,
> And peaceful leave before thy feet.
>
> In scenes exalted or depressed,
> Thou art our joy, and thou our rest;
> Thy goodness all our hopes shall raise,
> Adored through all our changing days.

Like the other children in the family, Doddridge was frail from the day of his birth, and it was remarkable that he lived as long as he did. Rapidly sinking with consumption, he sought the milder climate of Portugal. But it was too late; he died on October 26, 1751, and was buried in the English cemetery at Lisbon. When Charles Wesley heard the sad news he was deeply affected. Hurriedly writing to his intimate friend, George Whitefield, he exclaimed: "Doddridge is dead! we must begin, we must begin!"

"I went to church. I gave a shilling; and seeing a poor girl at the sacrament in a bed-gown, I gave her privately half a crown, though I saw Hart's hymns in her hand." Thus wrote Samuel Johnson, kind-souled, but evidently no admirer of Hart. This Joseph Hart was born in London in 1712, and for many years he was a teacher. The son of devout parents, he himself did not become a Christian till he was forty-five. He was sincere but morbid. He tells us what a "monstrous sinner" he had been; his "gloomy, dreadful state;" the "doleful hours spent in solitude and sorrow." And then at the Pentecost of 1757 he was blessedly converted. Though to the end of his days "the buffetings of Satan . . . and clouds and darkness" continued to torment him, he enjoyed much comfort, and it was during the two years following his conversion that most of his more than two hundred hymns were written.

Yielding to the importunity of friends, he entered the ministry, and for eight years, till his death in 1768, he was the pastor of an Independent chapel. His hymns are fast disappearing from our collections, to make way for later and better ones; but for a hundred years they were extremely popular, especially with churches of a Calvinistic bent. Though never reaching the standard of either Doddridge or Watts, their simple piety and glow of personal experience gave them a strong appeal to the England that was thirsty for real religion: The most unlettered worshiper could understand such lines as

> This, this is the God we adore,
>   Our faithful, unchangeable Friend;
> Whose love is as great as his power,
>   And neither knows measure nor end.
>
> 'Tis Jesus, the First and the Last,
>   Whose Spirit shall guide us safe home;
> We'll praise him for all that is past,
>   And trust him for all that's to come.

In spite of the fact that it is not addressed to God, but is merely an appeal of the converted to the unconverted, the old hymn, "Come, ye sinners, poor and wretched," has been sung with blessed results times without number. Whatever Hart may have been as a poet, he certainly had an immense following. It is related that on the day of his funeral no less than twenty thousand people thronged the Bunhill Fields Burial Ground. Appropriately his own hymn was sung:

> Earthly cavern, to thy keeping
>   We commit our Brother's dust;
> Keep it safely, softly sleeping,
>   Till our Lord demand thy trust.
>
> Sweetly sleep, dear Saint, in Jesus;
>   Thou, with us, shalt wake from Death;
> Hold he cannot, though he seize us;
>   We his power defy by faith.

We think of Joseph Addison as the charming essayist, so critical of his diction that he would have stopped the press to change a preposition. But he was more than this. The son of the Dean of Lichfield, and nephew of the Bishop of Bristol, he grew up in a churchly atmosphere. His education was the finest that Oxford could afford, and later he married the Countess of Warwick. With easy grace he moved in the highest social circles, and he soon came to occupy an important place in the public life of England. Best of all, in an age notorious for its loose morals, he preserved an unblemished character. He was known not merely for his varied accomplishments, but also as a devout Christian gentleman.

Addison the hymn writer is remembered not for quantity, but for quality. Readers of "The Spectator" in 1712 were probably amazed to find six essays, appearing at intervals, each of which contained a hymn. All were anonymous, but we know that one was by Watts and the others by Addison. Of these latter, the first is a rendering of the Twenty-third Psalm. Still better known, however, is the stately hymn, "The spacious firmament on high," inspired by the words, "The heavens declare the glory of God; and the firmament showeth his handiwork." As wedded to the beautiful strains from Haydn's "Creation," it almost reaches the proportions of an anthem. The hymn beginning,

> How are thy servants blest, O Lord!
> How sure is their defense,

was a reminiscence from the poet's travels, years before. During a voyage on the Mediterranean a storm arose so violent that even the captain gave up all hope. Mingled fear and gratitude breathe in the lines,

> When by the dreadful tempest borne
> High on the broken wave,
> They know thou art not slow to hear,
> Nor impotent to save.

> The storm is laid, the winds retire,
>   Obedient to thy will;
> The sea, that roars at thy command,
>   At thy command is still.

Best known and loved of Addison's hymns is the one sung everywhere:

> When all thy mercies, O my God,
>   My rising soul surveys.

These hymns appeared five years after Watts's famous little volume of 1707, and quite possibly they were suggested by that earlier collection. But Addison was in no sense an imitator of Watts. He was his own master. If his hymns lack in spiritual glow, they have the literary grace and the quiet sincerity we should expect from such a pen. They are among the comparatively few written by laymen. They are truly devotional, the language of one who could say, as the end drew near: "See in what peace a Christian can die."

VIII

THE WESLEY HYMNS

THE PROTESTANT REFORMATION, as we have seen, gave rise to two streams of Christian song. The one had its source in French hearts—Clement Marot, Calvin and Beza—all of them at some time refugees in Switzerland, and it was confined to renderings of the psalms into French and English. From Geneva, the center of the Reformed Church, it crossed the Channel, gathering strength as it passed, and becoming a mighty tide in England and Scotland and afterward in the American Colonies. Later, hymns were introduced, but the hand of Geneva was on them, as we see in the songs of Watts and his followers.

The other stream rose in Bohemia, among the disciples of Huss, but far more in Germany, under Luther, and it chiefly affected hymnody. As it widened, it swept on among the Germanic peoples with irresistible force. For long years it found no place in England, till at last John Wesley discovered the power of Christian song on the Continent. He translated some of the best hymns into his mother tongue, and, still better, he carried the German spirit to his own land. Here it was caught up by the inspired Charles, and thence came the hymns of the Revival Period. With the passage of the years these two streams merged and today they flow on in one stately current of sacred praise.

If blood tells, John and Charles Wesley were highly favored, for their ancestry was the best. John was born on June 17, 1703, and Charles four and a half years later, December 18, 1707. The arrival of Charles was premature, and the tiny babe was tenderly wrapped in wool to protect the flickering life. The boys were reared with the wise care to be expected from a mother like Susannah Wesley. And then in due time they entered Oxford, which for generations had been the family university. For a while John was troubled by Charles's bent toward suspicious "diversions": "If I spoke to him about religion, he would warmly answer, 'What, would you have me to be a saint at once?' and would hear no more." But this soon passed, and presently we find the young men, both of them ordained in the Anglican ministry, on their way to the infant American colony of Georgia. John was to be parish priest, and Charles secretary to Governor Oglethorpe.

Among the immigrants were twenty-six Germans, all of them Moravians. During the long voyage they often sang the hymns of the Fatherland, which they loved so well; and when the seas roared their voices were loudest. Such faith, in contrast to his own timidity, impressed John in particular, and it set him to pondering as never before. In the small parcel of books which he took with him he carefully included Watts's "Psalms and Hymns," the more remarkable when we remember what a novelty such things were in those days, and that Watts was a Dissenter and Wesley a stiff Anglican churchman.

Evidently John's thoughts were stirring, and it was not in vain, for after reaching Georgia he prepared a small hymn book of his own. While nothing was from the pen of either John or Charles, half came from Watts, and still more to the point, it was the first hymn book compiled for use in the Church of England (Gregory, 155), the forerunner of the long series prepared by the Wesley brothers. In the spring of 1738 the men were back in London, and then occurred the religious crisis of their lives. On May 21, Charles Wesley was "converted," and three days later the blessing came to John, largely through Moravian example and influence.

Eager for still more light, and already familiar with German, John hurried on to Herrnhut, the famous Moravian center. Never had he heard such singing as now, and no sooner was he home than he began that series of matchless translations into English of some of the best German hymns. Still better, he gave his blessing to the gifted

Charles as "the sweet singer" of the new religious movement. Nor was there anything strange in this impulse toward sacred song. For long years the poetic bent had been in the Wesley family. The father of John and Charles had penned the "Life of Christ" in verse, which was highly regarded in those days, and the older brother, Samuel, was a poet of no mean parts. Moreover, in religious song it was a time of leanness. The old metrical psalms had lost their savor, and though their use was a part of the daily routine in the Epworth Rectory, even Susannah Wesley could never interest her children in them. It was still worse in church. Years afterward, speaking of his boyhood John told of the "drawl of a parish clerk, the screaming of boys who bawl out what they neither feel nor understand" (Tyerman, Life, 2:282). Clear it was that a spiritual revival was beyond hope unless singing lips kept beat with glowing hearts. Charles Wesley was a prophet as truly as John, and the sermons in verse far outpaced the sermons in prose.

Charles Wesley wrote more than six thousand hymns. Rarely was there conscious effort. He wrote because he must; breathing was no more natural. Doubtless the genius was already there, but in May, 1738, it suddenly burst into flame, and thenceforth every thought carried a poetic hue. Of his hymns the bulk were never used, and probably were never intended to be used in public worship. They were addressed to various living friends, or written in commemoration of the dead. Many were sung only at class meeting or on other semi-private occasions. Yet even so, he wrote far too much. His standard was high, and, without realizing it, again and again he fell below what he was capable of doing.

Now and then his good taste went astray. In speaking of things consistent with each other, why call then "consentaneous"? "A swoon of silent love," sounds far-fetched. Even the rapture of fellowship with God cannot excuse "He dandled me upon His knee." The glory of the Creator is not enhanced when the creature calls himself "a loathsome hypocrite," a "beast and devil," "an outward saint, a fiend within." Let us hope that Wesley never really felt this way about himself.

By far the keenest, as well as the kindest, critic Charles had was John. The brothers knew and appreciated each other, their strength and weakness, as no one else could. John describes Charles's hymns as: "Some bad, some mean, some most excellently good." He went still further and used the term "namby-pamby," and he was right. John could speak thus, but woe to any outside meddler who dared lay hand on those treasures. Neither one, especially John, would tolerate it. The brothers were a mutual admiration society. No wonder that Charles Wesley did not always tread the high places of sacred song. He was no superman. Like other mortals, he sometimes soared and again he drooped.

The surprising fact is that he rarely if ever fell below a certain point; the average was singularly high. It is well to remember that, with the different standards of the time, some things which we would avoid, were in another period quite appropriate. That was a controversial age. Calvinism and Arminianism were abroad in the land, armed to the teeth. When the sons of Geneva sang:

> We are a garden walled around,
> Chosen and made peculiar ground;
> A little spot enclosed by grace
> Out of the world's wide wilderness, (Gregory: 168)

Wesley's ire was stirred; and as for the doctrine that innocent babes are condemned to perdition from all eternity simply to enhance the divine glory—"hellish blasphemy," he called it—his metrical replies fairly quivered with indignation. But today, quite apart from the merits of the case, we are all agreed that religious song is no place for controversy.

Time was when hymns were entirely didactic. Those of Charles Wesley form a theological library on Christian truth. This was of untold value in an age when the mass of the people were densely ignorant of even the fundamentals of the faith. But there is danger. We fancy that the grimy miners, unable to read or write, must have been sadly puzzled as they sang from memory:

> God we in our Saviour see,
>   None beside himself we know;
> Christ the consubstantial Son,
>
> *　　*　　*　　*
>
> One with his eternal sire.
>
> (Osborne 7;220)

Even Charles Wesley sometimes forgot that doctrine in verse must be very simple.

In his hymns Wesley covered the whole sweep of human experience from the cradle to the grave. He sang of a "new-born child," "a sick child," "child in the smallpox," "a child cutting teeth." There were hymns for young people. The love letters he wrote to his future wife were in the form of hymns. The family physician had his hymns, also "all mankind," including Jews, Turks and heathen. Even the "lunatic and sore vexed" were not neglected. "Entering a house," "At lying down," "In weariness"—every event from sun to sun, as well as all the periods of life, and every sort of individual, hundreds, thousands—all were provided with their appropriate hymns. While this added an intenser human touch, it is needless to say that, with some exceptions, it made such hymns entirely unsuited to public use.

Speaking of children, it is interesting to know that Charles Wesley wrote not only *on* children, but *for* children. Unfortunately those hymns were not a success. The unmarried Watts did better than Wesley, the father of eight children. Some of the Wesley boys were prodigies, but all children are not prodigies, and perhaps the father forgot this, for most of his children's hymns were beyond the child mind. Only those of sedate years could properly sing,

> Let the potsherds of the earth
> Boast their virtues, beauty, birth;
> A poor, guilty worm I am,
> Ransomed by the bleeding Lamb.
>
> (Osborne 6;444)

Nor could rollicking boys and girls quite fathom the doom
which awaited their misbehaving companions:

> Dark and bottomless the pit
>   Which on them its mouth shall close;
> Never shall they 'scape from it;
>   There they shall in endless woes
> Weep, and wail, and gnash their teeth,
> Die an everlasting death. (Osborne 378)

What relief to turn to

> Gentle Jesus, meek and mild,
> Look upon a little child;
> Pity my simplicity,
> Suffer me to come to thee. (Osborne 6:441)

This is the first stanza in a series of fourteen. Would that
Wesley had always written like that, for then we would
crown him as the sweetest singer for children the Church
has ever known.

The outstanding quality of Charles Wesley's hymns is
expressed in the word "life." They throb, they fairly leap.
No quiet garden nook or classic study for him! The dusty
highway; the moor; the jostling crowd, uncouth, head-
strong, but always needy; even a mob; or perhaps the passion of an inner experience—here he found subject and
inspiration. Much of his best work was done on horseback.
His friend, Henry Moore, relates how "not infrequently he
has come to our house in the City Road, and having left the
pony in the garden in front, he would enter, crying out, 'Pen
and ink! pen and ink!' These being supplied, he wrote the
hymn he had been composing. When this was done, he
would look round on those present, and salute them with
much kindness, ask after their health, give out a short hymn,
and thus put all in mind of eternity." He yearned and
wrote for the spiritual needs of others, but his own experience set the pace. When he and John were converted, out
of newborn rapture sprang the words:

Where shall my wondering soul begin?
How shall I all to heaven aspire?
A slave redeemed from death and sin,
A brand plucked from eternal fire,
How shall I equal triumph raise,
And sing my great Deliverer's praise?
(Osborne 1;91)

On the first anniversary of his conversion Charles wrote:

O for a thousand tongues to sing
My great Redeemer's praise!

It was not a mere accident that so many of the supreme hymns date from the first two years after the new birth, such as, "Jesus, Lover of my soul;" "Depth of mercy! can there be;" "O for a thousand tongues to sing;" "Forever here my rest shall be;" and that matchless trio—"Hark! the herald angels sing;" "Christ the Lord is risen today;" and "Hail the day that sees him rise;" while only a few months later there appeared possibly the greatest of all, "Come, O thou traveler unknown." Those were the days when the spiritual glow was freshest, if not richest. The heart was too full for silence; no wonder it burst into song. How vividly personal the experience was constantly appears:

And can it be that I should gain
An interest in the Saviour's blood?
Died he for me, who caused him pain?
For me, who him to death pursued?
Amazing love! how can it be
That thou, my Lord, should'st die for me?

Such a person has a right to talk about love. Wesley sang of it thousands of times; he glorified it; he hungered for it; "O give me love, or else I die!" (Osborne 1:76). He never wrote a more characterisic hymn than "Jesus, Lover of my soul."

Wesley was saved, and with his whole being he yearned for others. This was the burden of his message in song:

O that the world might taste and see
The riches of his grace!

From every hand he drew suggestions; yet not from the halls of contemplation, but from the busy walks of men. He stood in the streets of Newcastle; crowds gathered and listened to the gospel story. It was winter, but, says he: "They had no feeling of the frost while the love of Christ warmed their hearts." And then he wrote:

> Ye neighbors and friends of Jesus draw near;
> His love condescends by titles so dear
> To call and invite you his promise to prove,
> And freely delight you in Jesus' love.

Again he fell into thanksgiving as he thought how divine grace had transformed the colliers of Kingswood, once wild as savage beasts:

> Glory to God, whose sovereign grace
>   Hath animated senseless stones,
> Called us to stand before his face,
>   And raised us into Abraham's sons.

He watched and pitied the swarming crowds in Moorfields, more silly than sheep:

> O all that pass by, to Jesus draw near;
> He utters a cry, ye sinners give ear!
> From hell to retrieve you, he spreads out his hands;
> Now, now to receive you, he graciously stands.

On one occasion he visited the western tip of England, and as he looked out from the dizzy cliffs of Land's End on the boisterous waves, he shuddered: "Where am I? An immortal soul?"

> Lo! on a narrow neck of land,
> 'Twixt two unbounded seas I stand,
>   Secure, insensible;
> A point of time, a moment's space,
> Removes me to that heavenly place,
>   Or shuts me up in hell.

The persecutions heaped upon the early Methodists, and often shared by the Wesley brothers, were brutality itself; but the sufferers were not forgotten at the throne of grace:

> Dear dying Lamb, for whom alone
>   We suffer pain, and shame and loss,
> Hear thine afflicted people groan,
>   Crushed by the burden of thy Cross,
> And bear our fainting spirits up,
> And bless the bitter, sacred cup.

Many a time, especially in the night watches, the poet lived over again the memorable voyage to far-away Georgia:

> Lord of the wide-extended main,
>   Whose power the winds and seas controls,
> Whose hand doth earth and heaven sustain,
>   Whose Spirit leads believing souls,
>
> Throughout the deep thy footsteps shine,
>   We own thy way is in the sea,
> O'erawed by Majesty Divine,
>   And lost in thy immensity.

Hundreds of hymns were inspired by occasions peculiarly dear to Methodists. The class meeting and love feast were made vocal with song:

> Come, and let us sweetly join
> Christ to praise in hymn divine;
> Give we all with one accord
> Glory to our common Lord;
> Hands, and hearts, and voices raise;
> Sing as in the ancient days,
> Antedate the joys above,
> Celebrate the Feast of Love.

The Watch Night service, lasting for hours, was memorable, and appealed to both saints and sinners. Some of the old songs will never pass out:

> Blow ye the trumpet, blow
>   The gladly solemn sound;
> Let all the nations know,
>   To earth's remotest bound,
> The year of jubilee is come;
> Return, ye ransomed sinners, home.

*   *   *   *

> Come, let us anew
> Our journey pursue,
> Roll round with the year
> And never stand still, till the Master appear,
> His adorable will let us gladly fulfill,
> And our talents improve,
> By the patience of hope, and the labor of love.

Unusual events were full of suggestion. The great Lisbon earthquake of 1775 filled men's hearts with terror. Charles Wesley was mightily stirred, and he wrote what Southey has declared to be the finest hymn in the English tongue, opening with the lines,

> Stand the Omnipotent decree!
> Jehovah's will be done!
> Nature's end we wait to see,
> And hear her final groan.
> Let this earth dissolve and blend
> In death the wicked and the just,
> Let those ponderous orbs descend,
> And grind us into dust.

Now and then, as an exception to the rule, a hymn might be suggested by a book. From the time he was a member of the Holy Club, Charles Wesley had known and loved Matthew Henry's "Commentary on the Bible." It had been his daily companion till the very language was absorbed and became a part of his thinking. In referring to Leviticus 8:35, "Ye shall keep the charge of the Lord," Henry said: "We have every one of us a charge to keep, an eternal God to glorify, an immortal soul to provide for—our generation to serve." From this it is interesting to turn to Wesley's lines,

> A charge to keep I have,
> A God to glorify,
> A never-dying soul to save,
> And fit it for the sky.
>
> *   *   *   *
>
> To serve the present age.

John Wesley could truly say, "Our people die well." He and Charles were at many death beds and they knew. There were tears, but they were more tears of joy. As the dead were carried to burial, the streets rang with shouts of victory. Said a physician to Charles Wesley, "Most people die for fear of dying; but I never met with such people as yours. They are none of them afraid of death, but calm and patient and resigned to the last." Charles Wesley's career on earth closed in his eighty-first year. He died as he had lived. As the end drew near, he called his wife to his side and from his lips she took the farewell message:

> In age and feebleness extreme,
> Who shall a helpless worm redeem?
> Jesus, my only hope thou art,
> Strength of my failing flesh and heart,
> O could I catch one smile from thee,
> And drop into eternity!

John and Charles were twin souls. A few days after the brother's death, John was preaching at Bolton. He gave out the hymn,

> Come, O thou Traveler unknown,
> Whom still I hold, but cannot see!
> My company before is gone,
> And I am left alone with thee.

As he reached the third line there swept over him a sense of his loss, and he burst into tears and sat down. The whole congregation wept in sympathy, and it was sometime before the service could proceed. Less than three years and John passed on. How beatific the reunion must have been!

Some of Charles's sweetest verse was written for funerals. To be sure, once he descended to "Ah lovely appearance of death!" but only once. With rare exceptions his hymns were in fine taste. Poor would the Church be without

> How happy every child of grace,
> Who knows his sins forgiven!
> This earth, he cries, is not my place,
> I seek my place in heaven;

or

> Come let us join our friends above
> That have obtained the prize;

or

> Rejoice for a brother deceased,
> Our loss is his infinite gain,

albeit sedate America changed "rejoice" to "weep not."

Charles Wesley and George Whitefield were lifelong friends, and when the news came that Whitefield had died, Wesley was stricken with grief. His feelings burst out in those noble lines of mingled sorrow and triumph, beginning,

> Servant of God, well done!
> Thy glorious warfare's past;
> The battle's fought, the race is won,
> And thou art crowned at last.

IX

OTHER 18TH CENTURY HYMNISTS

ISAAC WATTS was not unfriendly to the revival movement under the Wesleys, but he came too early to be
caught up in the tide that was sweeping England; and,
more than that, temperamentally he preferred quiet ways.
For years after Methodism began the hymns of Charles
Wesley were written expressly for his own people, and were
sung by them almost exclusively. This gave them a sectarian tone, which hindered the more general use they afterward attained. Naturally other hymn writers of the eighteenth century were divided. Some followed Watts. Others,
coming under the spell of the new evangelism, quite apart
from theological belief, and ofttimes unwittingly, fell into the
train of Charles Wesley.

It is interesting to know that the most prominent hymn
writer the Baptists have given to the Church was a woman, a
woman born more than two hundred years ago, when women
writers of any kind were few and woman herself was at a
discount. In the English village of Broughton, where Anne
Steele (1716-1778) lived, the Baptists were a humble folk,
and her father, who was a lumber merchant, served as pastor
of the local church without salary for sixty years. Reared
in such a home of religious devotion, it was no wonder that
Anne grew up a consecrated Christian girl. When a mere
child she learned to use her pen, and on occasion she would
entertain her companions with bits of poetry.

Then came hymns, but her modesty held them back, and
not till she was a woman of fifty-four were they published,
one hundred and forty-four in number. Her friends everywhere were delighted. Now, at last, what Watts and Doddridge and Wesley had done for other branches of the Church
was being done for the Baptists. Rapidly the new hymns

found their way among Dissenters, and also with Anglicans of evangelical spirit. When Trinity Church, Boston, decided on a hymn book of its own, of one hundred and fifty-two selections, fifty-nine were by Miss Steele (Benson's "The English Hymn"; p. 214.) She led the way in that distinguished line of woman hymnists which will never end.

Miss Steele's hymns are not only devout, and perfectly simple and natural in expression, but running through them is a tender, plaintive note, a reaction from her own experience. When a child she met with an accident which crippled her for life; and worse was to follow. She became engaged to be married and the time was set. Her lover, a noble young fellow, spent the previous day with her in joyous anticipation. At evening he left, to bathe in a neighboring stream, and there he was drowned. No wonder that her hair turned gray and youth faded from her cheeks. Accumulated sorrow would have utterly crushed some girls or made them cynics. Anne Steele bore up with singular resignation, but an indelible impress was made on her hymns. We feel it as we sing:

> Father, whate'er of earthly bliss
> Thy sovereign will denies,
> Accepted at thy throne of grace,
> Let this petition rise.
>
> Give me a calm, a thankful heart,
> From every murmur free;
> The blessings of thy grace impart,
> And make me live to thee.

She had no morbid desire to be done with this world, yet at times she wistfully thought of how,

> Far from these narrow scenes of night,
> Unbounded glories rise,
> And realms of joy and pure delight,
> Unknown to mortal eyes.
>
> Fair, distant land!—could mortal eyes
> But half its charms explore,
> How would our spirits long to rise
> And dwell on earth no more!

> O may the heavenly prospect fire
>   Our hearts with ardent love,
> Till wings of faith, and strong desire,
>   Bear every thought above.

Faith, hope, joy, all were sustained by her consuming devotion to the Master. She was constantly singing his praise, as in the familiar lines,

> Come, ye that love the Saviour's name,
>   And joy to make it known,
> The Sovereign of your Hearts proclaim,
>   And bow before his throne.

and again,

> To our Redeemer's glorious Name
>   Awake the sacred song;
> O may his love—immortal flame—
>   Tune every heart and tongue.

This devotion was the very heart and soul of her Christian experience.

In 1739 John Wesley wrote to a friend: "At Reading I found a young man,—Cennick by name—willing to suffer, yea, to die for his Lord." The "young man" was twenty-one at the time and the very type that Wesley needed. He eagerly followed the great evangelist and became the first lay preacher that Methodism ever had. Unhappily he was vacillating. The record of his brief career of thirty-six years shows that he was born a Quaker; he grew up in the Church of England; for a while he was with Wesley, and then he shifted to Whitefield, finally becoming a Moravian.

But he never lost his early devotion to the Master. Not a great hymnist, he has a definite place of his own. The lines on the returning Christ are crude, but they show lyric power:

> Lo! He cometh, countless trumpets
>   Blow before his bloody sign!
> 'Midst ten thousand saints and angels,
>   See the Crucified shine.
>   Alleluiah!
> Welcome, welcome, bleeding Lamb!

The most widely sung of John Cennick's hymns is

> Children of the Heavenly King,
> As ye journey, sweetly sing;
> Sing your Saviour's worthy praise,
> Glorious in his works and ways.

Even more popular with the Methodist fathers, especially in "experience" meetings, and still sung with great gusto, is

> Jesus, my all to heaven is gone,
> He whom I fix my hopes upon.

The best-known lines that Cennick ever wrote, and which, in spite of the young man's wanderings, appealed so strongly to John Wesley that he constantly used them, and had them engraved on his family teapot, were the two "Graces before and after Meat"; the one,

> Be present at our table, Lord!
> Be here and everywhere adored;
> Thy creatures bless and grant that we
> May feast in Paradise with thee.

And the other, beginning,

> We bless thee, Lord! for this our food,
> But more for Jesus' flesh and blood.

Thomas Olivers (1725-1799) was a diamond, but decidedly rough. As a youth he was apprenticed to a shoemaker, but he soon became so wild and dissolute that he lost his job. One evening he saw a crowd flocking to a chapel and in curiosity he went with the rest. There, under the spell of such an appeal as he had never heard before, he was converted—one of the many trophies won by George Whitefield. Later he became a life-long follower of John Wesley. He did not write much, but in a moment of inspiration he gave to the Church a hymn of unique merit. The idea was already running through his mind, when, one Friday night, he dropped in at the Jewish synagogue in London, and heard Leoni, the priest, chant a Hebrew doxology. The melody caught his ear; he asked for a copy, and to this he wrote the words, "The God of Abraham praise," calling the tune "Leoni." The unusual meter renders it less singable than most hymns, but we agree with Montgomery's verdict that "there is not in our language a lyric of more majestic style." The opening stanza is typical of the whole:

> The God of Abraham praise,
>   Who reigns enthroned above;
> Ancient of everlasting days,
>   And God of love;
> Jehovah, Great I AM,
>   By earth and heaven confessed;
> I bow and bless the sacred name,
>   Forever blessed.

Eight years after John Wesley was buried in the graveyard of City Road Chapel, the tomb was opened, and the body of Thomas Olivers was laid beside that of the man whom so long he had loved and revered.

Like many others Edward Perronet would be utterly unknown, had he not written a hymn. Nine out of ten who sing with joy and profit, "All hail the power of Jesus' name," have no idea who composed it. Perronet was descended from the refugees who fled from France in the unhappy days of Louis XIV. His father, Vincent, became a minister in the Anglican Church, and to the very close of his remarkable life of ninety-one years he was a flaming Evangelical. It was supposed that Edward would follow right on, but he was too sensitive to the faults of the Established Church, "tottering communion," he called it, adding "I despise her nonsense."

Like his father in evangelistic fervor, he held for a time to John Wesley, facing any mob (as Wesley said), and enduring being "thrown down and rolled in mud and mire." But he was too independent for human leadership, and the closing years of his life were spent as pastor of a small Congregational chapel in Canterbury. Perronet's great hymn was written about 1779. A twenty-year-old friend of musical bent, Shrubsole by name, saw the manuscript and composed a tune which was afterward used at a chapel in Miles

Lane, London; hence a title that has clung ever since. By common consent this hymn is one of the greatest ever written. With dramatic power it portrays the scene following the resurrection when heaven and earth do homage to the triumphant Christ; when from the four winds they come in turn, angels, Jews, sinners, every kindred, and, gathering around the throne, "Crown him Lord of all." Perronet was buried in the cloisters of Canterbury Cathedral. His last words typified the man:

> Glory to God in the height of his divinity!
> Glory to God in the depth of his humanity!
> Glory to God in his all-sufficiency!
> Into his hand I commend my spirit.

Scattered through the years are the names of writers, none of them of outstanding merit, and yet to all of whom we are indebted. Sometimes it is with gratitude for a single hymn, but perhaps that hymn through long use and tender association has endeared itself to the whole Church. We think of the Welshman, William Williams, born in 1717. When the movement under Whitefield swept through Wales, Williams was drawn into it, and for thirty-five years, like a flaming torch, he went from place to place among his native hills, holding revival meetings. He has been called "the sweet singer of Wales." He wrote hundreds of pieces, all of them in the Welsh tongue. A few found their way into English. The one we know and love the best is:

> Guide me, O thou great Jehovah,
> Pilgrim through this barren land.

The lips of Williams have long been silent, but pilgrims to the heavenly Canaan have never ceased to sing his prayer of faith and trust.

There was Joseph Grigg, who died in 1768 when barely forty years of age. He was a Presbyterian minister, a fact long since forgotten, but we can never forget that he wrote those tender lines of warning and appeal:

Behold a Stranger at the door!
He gently knocks, has knocked before;
Has waited long, is waiting still;
You treat no other friend so ill.

From the same pen we have that other hymn, still more familiar, beginning,

Jesus, and shall it ever be,
A mortal man ashamed of thee?

Persistent tradition assures us that this second hymn was written when the author was only ten years old. But whatever his age, the Church received a treasure of enduring worth.

Robert Robinson was born in 1735. He came from a humble home and his prospects in life were so poor that he was thankful to become an apprentice to a hairdresser. But God had other plans. When a lad of sixteen, he drifted into a service where George Whitefield was the preacher. As he afterwards confessed, "It was to spy the nakedness of the land I came, to pity the folly of the preacher, the infatuation of the hearers, and to abhor the doctrine." But the sermon struck home and led to his conversion. In time he became pastor of the Baptist church at Cambridge, preceding the celebrated Robert Hall. Not contented with his immediate parish, he spent the leisure hours in the highways and hedges, seeking the lost, quite willing to be dubbed the "Bishop of Barns and Fields." He also found time, now and then, to write a bit of verse to be sung. In spite of its confused metaphors, we would be loath to part with that hymn of the fathers, "Come, thou fount of every blessing." Robinson has poured into it his own experience, as when he tells us:

Jesus sought me when a stranger,
Wandering from the fold of God;
He, to rescue me from danger,
Interposed his precious blood.

Superior to this is that other hymn,

> Mighty God! while angels bless thee,
> May a mortal lisp thy name?

Few sacred songs have more majesty than this; it added dignity to the most churchly service.

Only eternity will reveal the indebtedness of the Church to George Whitefield. Among the spiritual trophies of that mighty evangelist was John Fawcett, converted when a mere lad, whose life covered the long stretch from 1739 to 1817. For several years Fawcett went with the Methodists and then he joined the Baptists and became a minister in that communion. As was more or less the custom in those days, he often summed up the leading ideas of his sermons "in a few plain verses," to be sung at the close of the service. Thus it is that we have a number of hymns from his pen, not of the first grade, but deeply spiritual. Very fittingly a sermon on the Bible was followed by the words,

> How precious is the book divine,
>   By inspiration given!
> Bright as a lamp its doctrines shine,
>   To guide our souls to heaven.

Probably no hymn is more often sung, and more popular for its simplicity than "Blest be the tie that binds." There seems to be much truth in the familiar tradition that, after Fawcett had been pastor for several years of a small church in Yorkshire, he accepted a call to a more important pulpit in London. The farewell sermon had been preached and the loaded wagons were ready to start with the furniture. The broken-hearted parishioners were gathered for the "goodbyes," when Mrs. Fawcett burst out: "O John, John, I cannot bear this! I know not how to go!" "Nor I, either," was the reply. "Nor will we go; unload the wagons, and put everything in the place where it was before." From this experience grew the hymn on mutual love. Certainty is impossible, but it is more than likely that we are also indebted to John Fawcett for that most appropriate closing hymn, probably often used by his own people:

> Lord, dismiss us with thy blessing,
> Fill our hearts with joy and peace.

We think of Anna Laetitia Barbauld as belonging to the eighteenth century, though her life of eighty-two years did not close till 1825. She was an unusual woman. A clergyman's daughter and a clergyman's wife, trained in the classics as well as other branches, a writer of literary grace and vigor, with a pen always busy in prose or poetry, she probably was surpassed by no woman of her time in general culture. It is refreshing to turn from some of the verses of those days to the refined lines of Mrs. Barbauld. She is classified with the Unitarians, but we are well contented to sing:

> "Come," said Jesus' sacred voice,
> "Come and make my path your choice;
> I will guide you to your home;
> Weary pilgrim, hither come."

Her hymn on "The Death of the Virtuous" has been a favorite at a multitude of funerals:

> How blest the righteous when he dies!
>   When sinks a weary soul to rest,
> How mildly beams the closing eyes,
>   How gently heaves the expiring breast!
>
> *   *   *   *
>
> Life's labor done, as sinks the clay,
>   Light from its load the spirit flies,
> While heaven and earth combine to say,
>   "How blest the righteous when he dies!"

The best thing she ever wrote is that exquisite gem, perfect of its kind, but unhappily not to be sung:

> Life! we've been long together,
> Through pleasant and through cloudy weather;
> 'Tis hard to part when friends are dear—
> Perhaps 'twill cost a sigh, a tear;
> Then steal away, give little warning,
>   Choose thine own time;
>   Say not "Goodnight," but in a brighter clime
> Bid me "Good Morning."

Some people soar only once, but they rise so high that the once is enough. Toplady's sermons are no longer read. Of his one hundred and thirty-three hymns, one hundred and thirty-two are rarely sung. His theological polemics long since went to the scrapheap. But the writing of "Rock of Ages" has sufficed to place him among the immortals.

Augustus Montague Toplady was born in England in 1740. He never knew his father, who was a major in the British Army and who died in battle when the baby was a few weeks old. When a lad of sixteen, Augustus went with his mother on a visit to Ireland. One evening, curiosity drew him to a meeting, held in a barn where a crowd of peasants had gathered and a Methodist layman was preaching. But that primitive appeal led the boy to Christ. The years passed and we find Toplady back in England, a minister in the Anglican Church. He was in sympathy with John Wesley's evangelical spirit, but he abhorred the Wesleyan theology, for he had become an intense Calvinist. Again and again he assailed Wesley in the bitterest terms, declaring that his "satanic guilt" was equaled only by his "satanic shamelessness," and adding for himself that his one regret was that his language had not been even more severe. As we think of John Wesley's character and standing and the fact that he was thirty-seven years the senior, all this seems very strange. But it was a disputatious age. Toplady died at thirty-eight. Had he lived, his unnatural ardor would have cooled. He was the soul of sincerity, but he misunderstood some of the Wesleyan teachings. We do well to ignore the whole matter. At heart the two men were one. It is significant that the hymn book prepared by Toplady included a number of Charles Wesley's hymns, and there, side by side, are "Rock of Ages" and "Jesus, Lover of my Soul."

Toplady was a lover of sacred song. He sang in his own study; and often at night, instead of sleeping, he would put on his surplice and pace the garden by the hour, singing hymns. He himself wrote many, but we speak of only one. He was familiar with Charles Wesley's hymns and doubtless had read the lines, "What can the Rock of Ages move" and "Rock of Israel, cleft for me," and possibly these suggested his own opening words. Singularly, his hymn was written with a polemical purpose. He had an idea that John believed that sinners could atone in whole or in part for their own wrongdoing. In reply to such a false notion he penned what he called "A Living and Dying Prayer for the Holiest Believer in the World," in which he commended to the purest saint the language,

> In my hand no price I bring;
> Simply to thy Cross I cling.

The hymn appeared for the first time in March, 1776, in the "Gospel Magazine." The stanzas have been dissected to the last word and all manner of literary defects have been exposed. But the verdict of the years remains unchanged, that for congregational use this is supreme among English hymns. Simple enough for a child, profound enough for a patriarch, it expresses in the most appealing form the very heart of our common faith. In palace as well as cottage its comfort has been felt. We read of how its words were on the dying lips of Albert, consort of Victoria. Much later, following the death of Prince Albert Victor, eldest son of Edward VII, his mother, Alexandra, told how "in 1888 all my five children received the Holy Communion with me, and I gave Eddy a little book, and wrote in it:

> Nothing in my hand I bring,
> Simply to thy Cross I cling.

When he was gone, and lay like one sleeping, we laid a crown of flowers on his breast, and after we had done so, I turned to the table at his bedside, and saw the little book in which were written these words; and I could not help feeling that he did cling to the Cross, and that all had come true."

X

COWPER AND NEWTON

MONTGOMERY ONCE SAID that all sorts of people write hymns, except poets, and the words are truer than we wish. But William Cowper is a luminous exception. None will deny his poetical gifts, and from that same pen have come some of our best-loved hymns. Frail of body, unstable in mind, a peculiar pathos enshrouds his life. His father was a clergyman of standing in the Church of England, but it was the mother who bequeathed to him that delicate refinement of soul which always marked his conduct. She died when he was only six, but her memory was sacred. He could never speak of her without tears. From childhood he was subject to periods of melancholia, and as the years went by the attacks became more frequent and serious. They assumed the form of religious mania. He fancied he had committed the unpardonable sin, and again and again he attempted suicide. Happily he had devoted friends and none closer than John Newton, vicar of the parish church in the village of Olney. The two men became inseparable, and whenever health permitted Cowper acted as a sort of curate, visiting the sick and afflicted and frequently taking charge of the weekly service of prayer.

While thus engaged Newton proposed that they jointly prepare a hymn book. Not only would it serve parish needs, but it would provide easy diversion for Cowper. In this way, in 1779, the "Olney Hymns" made their appearance— three hundred and forty-eight in number, of which sixty-seven were by Cowper. From the beginning they were a great success. Though itself rarely used as a regular hymn book, the collection, from that day to this, has furnished rich material to compilers of other hymn books. Cowper's hymns breathe his own experience, and while they are rarely gloomy, they often sound a plaintive note which gives them a peculiar appeal. In extreme modesty he contrasts himself with the sainted Enoch, "O for a closer walk with God," and in the lines that follow we have the wistfulness that only the most sensitive soul can feel:

> Where is the blessedness I knew,
> When first I saw the Lord?
> Where is the soul-refreshing view
> Of Jesus and his word?

Again, he speaks to a "poor sinner," and in utter self-abasement he identifies himself with the sinner. In so doing he gives us one of the most touching appeals in the whole range of hymnody:

> Hark, my soul! It is the Lord;
> 'Tis thy Saviour, hear his word;
> Jèsus speaks, he speaks to thee;
> "Say, poor sinner, lov'st thou me?"

If Cowper had been living in these days, it is unlikely that he would have written the first stanza of "There is a fountain filled with blood," as we now have it. He would have used the same idea but in different language. And yet the hymn is such a perfect recital of his own experience and that of multitudes of others, it has been sung so often and gathered about it so many hallowed memories that, whether written in good taste or bad, it is sure of its place for years to come.

No hymn the poet gave us has a stronger hold on the heart of the Church than "God moves in a mysterious way;" but how few singers realize the mental and spiritual anguish amid which it was born. The exact circumstances no one knows, but it is connected with one of Cowper's attacks of religious mania when he nearly took his life. Yet, so skilfully is the merely personal concealed, that we sing the stanzas, thinking not of the writer, but taking fresh courage in new hope and faith. Some of his hymns have the simplest associations. For some time the weekly prayer meetings at Olney were held in cramped quarters, and when a larger room was provided no one was happier than Cowper. For the opening service he wrote the hymn,

> Jesus, where'er thy people meet,
> There they behold thy mercy-seat.

If Cowper now and then dropped into the dismal, there is no trace of it in the hymn beginning,

> Sometimes a light surprises
> The Christian while he sings.

Nothing of quiet trust is wanting in the closing stanza:

> Though vine and fig tree neither
> Their wonted fruit should bear,
> Though all the fields should wither,
> Nor flocks nor herds be there;
> Yet God the same abiding,
> His praise shall tune my voice;
> For while in him confiding,
> I cannot but rejoice.

A friend who looked upon Cowper after death could never forget how with the "composure and calmness" there "mingled, as it were, a holy surprise." As the mental cloud forever vanished, what visions of rapture he must have had!

We can never think of Cowper, the hymn writer, without including John Newton. This man was a miracle of divine grace. Left motherless when a child; a sailor in the merchant marine and then in the Royal Navy; deserting from a warship only to be caught and cruelly flogged; marooned for more than a year in Africa, where he was brutally treated by a slave dealer; again and again escaping the very jaws of death; so wicked that even sea captains were shocked and protested; and then, at the age of twenty-three signally converted—such, in a word, was one of the strangest of careers.

The human influence which above all else saved him from utter ruin was his passionate love for Mary Catlett, the girl who finally became his wife. Their love began when he was seventeen and she a child of thirteen. Neither could forget the other. After his conversion, he was for six years in the slave trade for himself, a respectable calling in those days. And then his thoughts turned to the ministry; but he was nearly forty before he was ordained and settled in his first parish at Olney. Here, as we have seen, that famous collection of hymns was issued. Happily Newton was modest; he well knew how inferior he was to Cowper in poetic talent. And yet, in full justice, it must be said that when the best hymns of the two men are placed side by side, Newton does not suffer in comparison. We say, the best, for much of the time Newton was not at his best. It is hard to understand how one day he could rush among the peaks, singing the noble strains,

> Glorious things of thee are spoken,
> Zion, city of our God,

and the next day he could tamely relate how

> The ice and snow we lately saw,
> Which covered all the ground,
> Are melted soon before the thaw,
> And can no more be found.

Newton's own vivid experience is reflected in many of his hymns. There is nothing borrowed in the lines,

> Amazing grace! how sweet the sound,
> That saved a wretch like me!
> I once was lost, but now am found;
> Was blind, but now I see.

Beatific as had been his change from death unto life, at times the shadows persisted in returning to plague him. There is nothing fanciful in his account of

> How tedious and tasteless the hours
> When Jesus no longer I see,

and many a struggling soul knows the pathos of the cry,

> Say, why do I languish and pine?
> And why are my winters so long?

At times all Pauline assurance seemed to depart and Newton fell into lugubrious phrase:

> 'Tis a point I long to know,
>   Oft it causes anxious thought;
> Do I love the Lord or no?
> Am I saved or am I not?

Again he would soar. Can we ask for anything more triumphant than this:

> When life sinks apace, and death is in view,
> The word of his grace shall comfort me through;
> Not fearing or doubting with Christ on our side,
> We hope to die shouting, "The Lord will provide!"

When a little company gathered in the prayer room on Saturday evening, they often sang the hymn especially written for the occasion:

> Safely through another week,
>   God has brought us on our way.

Some words seem too exquisitely tender for ordinary occasions. We feel this as we sing:

> How sweet the name of Jesus sounds
>   In a believer's ear;

one of the loveliest hymns ever written in honor of the "Name which is above every name."

In these days less is made than formerly of the passing of the Old Year, and naturally most of our hymns on this theme date from an earlier day. Newton never wrote anything in quite the solemn and stately measure of his "Time How Swift":

> While with ceaseless course, the sun
>   Hasted through the former year,
> Many souls their race have run,
>   Never more to meet us here.

When Newton became an old man and almost blind, friends urged him to give up preaching. "What!" he cried; "shall the old African blasphemer stop while he can speak!" So on he went to the end, and thus he died.

XI

NOTES ON 19TH CENTURY HYMNISTS

*(The following excerpts are from a lecture delivered
at Collegeville in the summer of 1925)*

ALL THROUGH the eighteenth century, the writing of hymns was almost exclusively in the hands of Nonconformists. The Anglicans regarded with lofty dsapproval such unchurchly activities and with dignified regularity went on their way singing the psalms in the well-approved rendering of Tate and Brady. But to the more discerning the rapid growth of the dissenting bodies showed unmistakably that their program of worship possessed elements of appeal which were sadly lacking in the Established Church. It became clear even to the conservative that the Church must either adopt hymn singing, or lose much of its hold on the people. And so it came about that a very remarkable change took place, and during the nineteenth century, while Nonconformists produced many worthy writers, the greatest hymnists were of the Anglican fold.

One of the earliest of this group was Reginald Heber, the great, beloved Bishop of Calcutta, who died in 1826, at the age of forty-three. As a minister in England, before his missionary days, he sorely felt the need of a good collection of hymns, and he proceeded to prepare one, he himself contributing no less than fifty-seven. While fault has been found with his hymns on the ground that he over-emphasizes the mere poetic element, the popular verdict has been so decidedly favorable that at the present time almost all of his hymns are in common use, which is unique in hymnody. The finest from his pen is that majestic anthem, "Holy, Holy, Holy, Lord God Almighty," echoing the phrase of the ancient prophets. Perhaps his best known is the great missionary hymn, "From Greenland's icy mountains." Singularly enough, this was written several years before he went to India as a missionary.

Henry Kirke White, who died in 1806 at the early age of twenty-one, is one of the small company of real poets who have contributed to hymnody. Excessive devotion to mathematical study led to his untimely decease. On the back of one of his study papers was found the hymn beginning, "Much in sorrow, oft in woe." Other hymns from this same pen are, "The Lord, our God, is clothed with might" and "When marshaled on the nightly plain." We cannot help wondering what this genius might have produced had he been spared to a normal age.

We owe a debt of gratitude to Sir John Bowring for his noble hymn, "In the cross of Christ I glory," which has been appropriated by the Church in many lands. How few people who sing it realize it was written by a Unitarian. Sir John also has given us, "Watchman, tell us of the night," "God is love; his mercy brightens" and other favorites.

John Keble's "Christian Year" has great merits and great defects, but all admit it contains some hymns of highest excellence. We at once think of his morning hymn, "New every morning is the love, Our wakening and uprising prove," and his still more familiar evening hymn, "Sun of my soul, thou Saviour dear."

Assuredly it was in a moment of inspiration that Henry Lyte, face to face with fast approaching death, penned the lines, "Abide with me, fast falls the eventide." Charlotte Elliott's "Just as I am, without one plea," the tender utterance of a personal experience, finds a place in almost all hymnals. To another woman, who was also a Unitarian, Sarah Flower Adams, we are indebted for that hymn which holds a merited place among the most popular in our tongue, "Nearer, my God, to thee."

We are glad that Henry Alford turned aside from his Greek studies long enough to write "Come, ye thankful people, come," perhaps the most popular hymn we have for

Thanksgiving Day; likewise that grand lyric, "Ten thousand times ten thousand, In sparkling raiment bright."

Nor do we forget the many noble hymns from Roman Catholic pens; Faber's "Faith of our fathers," "There's a wideness in God's mercy" and others; also Newman's matchless hymn, written in an hour of deep spiritual perplexity, as he was leaving the Church of his childhood and seeking rest in a new fold, "Lead, kindly Light."

These and very many other hymn writers make a great and goodly choir, each worthily uttering the praises of our God and of his Christ. Every true hymn is a Psalm of Life; running through it is the experimental note; and in the deeper things of the spirit there is a strange and blessed unity. It may be that in the providence of God the Songs of the Sanctuary are to have a larger part than we have sometimes thought in drawing together into the bonds of an enduring fellowship the people of God, until that day when, with unclouded vision, we shall gather around the great White Throne, and with angels and archangels and all the host of the redeemed sing the song of Moses and the Lamb.

Printed in the United States of America